T0171694

# TAKE ME BACK TO REDWAY

*Yolanda Strock Taylor*

**iUniverse, Inc.**
New York   Bloomington

*iUniverse books may be ordered through booksellers or by contacting:*

*iUniverse
1663 Liberty Drive
Bloomington, IN 47403
www.iuniverse.com
1-800-Authors (1-800-288-4677)*

*Because of the dynamic nature of the Internet, any Web addresses or
links contained in this book may have changed since publication and
may no longer be valid. The views expressed in this work are solely those
of the author and do not necessarily reflect the views of the publisher,
and the publisher hereby disclaims any responsibility for them.*

*ISBN: 978-1-4401-6706-5 (sc)
ISBN: 978-1-4401-6708-9 (hc)
ISBN: 978-1-4401-6707-2 (ebook)*

*Printed in the United States of America*

*iUniverse rev. date: 11/09/2009*

# Introduction

Take Me Back to Redway is the rags to riches memoir of a mother who lived the American dream. The story that is told weaves back and forth between the past (Yolanda as a child) and the present (Yolanda as an adult), with common themes connecting the two stories. The story begins with Yolanda as a child, suddenly alone with her father in Northern California, after escaping her abusive mother in Vietnam. The descriptions of the lifestyle of a homeless father and daughter, and the many associated challenges, is quickly overwhelmed by the strong father/daughter bond that is evident. The relationship that develops between father and daughter help to mold an individual with a fierce determination to succeed. The child who scrapes coins off the floor of the local laundromat, challenging neighborhood children to running races for a quarter a race, becomes the teenager who puts in 100 hour work weeks to save for an Ivy League education, and ultimately the adult who achieves her every childhood dream of success. When Yolanda is faced with her ultimate challenge, that of motherhood, she reflects on her past, longing for the simplicity of poverty, attempting to instill in her own children values of hard work and determination in an environment entirely distinct from the one she grew up in.

Take Me Back to Redway draws on the general interest in inspiring rags to riches stories. The author in Take Me Back to Redway learns to thrive despite the challenges of a very difficult childhood. In Take Me Back to Redway, father and daughter escape Vietnam and an abusive and neglectful mother. The mother finds them nine years later, with a painful year spent in custody court; readers fear the powerful father daughter combination will be broken apart. A stepmother enters the picture when Yolanda is ten; Yolanda resents her for stealing her father's attention, attention she realizes is invaluable in her development.

Yolanda's determination leaves readers cheering for her every success. She takes on three paper routes at once, starting at 4:30 am to finish before school. She learns it is quicker to run the route, taking multiple trips with only what she can carry. The morning hours spent running land her the top spot on the track team. To pay for college, she balances four jobs at once. After graduating near the top of her class from an Ivy League institution, Yolanda is determined to work on Wall Street, where she knows she can fulfill her long held dreams of financial security.

Take Me Back to Redway appeals to mothers who struggle with the balance between career and family. Countless stories are told of the chaos involved in trying to be successful at both work and parenting. Six months pregnant, Yolanda trips while running to catch a flight for work, almost terminating her pregnancy. Determined to not give up, she travels and works long hours, trying to prove she can do it all. In the end she decides to do what her father had done for her, and gives up her career to become a full time mom.

As a mother, although Yolanda hasn't figured out the right recipe in raising successful children, she is confident in the value of love, the value of spending as much time as possible with children when they are young, and the value in believing in them to give them the necessary self-confidence to succeed. All of these elements were present in her upbringing, and she wants to give the same to her children.

Take Me Back to Redway was written as a tribute to Yolanda's father, to recognize the incredible challenges he overcame as a single parent living in poverty. It was written for the many mothers who struggle over how best to raise their children, both for career moms and stay at home moms, and regardless of income class.

# Part 1

# Chapter 1 – Addictions and Impulsions

Although I was well aware he had been following me for miles, I was completely caught off guard when his bike pulled alongside mine. I had been glancing back every hundred yards or so, hoping he would turn a different way as I followed my daily route. I was a fast biker, but as hard as I tried to crank my pedals, he continued to close the ground between us. I had no time to react when he reached out, his right arm hitting me with a sudden blow. I flew off my bike, landing at the far edge of the overpass. I glanced down several hundred feet to the traffic below, looking at the cars that had no way of hearing my cries. I didn't notice the blood already oozing from my knees.

Instinctively, I jumped to my feet and began flailing my arms and screaming. "Help! Help!" I knew it was a worthless effort; there were no houses for miles, and after riding the same deserted stretch daily for weeks, I knew the odds of a car coming along anytime soon were slim.

I momentarily thought of my dad and his insistence that I not take a babysitting job so far from home.

"But the pay is really good. And it's fine, I can buy a bike and get there myself." I had argued.

"But what will you do when it rains? You know I won't

be able to ever drive you. Can't you find something closer to home?"

"But this family wants me fifty hours a week. I can't pass that up."

My dad insisted that I could find several jobs in town that would make just as much money, but I had already tried unsuccessfully for weeks, and I wasn't willing to miss more of the prime summer.

He gave up eventually, knowing I always did what I wanted in the end. I would make one hundred dollars a week, as much as I was making with my paper routes. I bought a bike at the police auction for five dollars and biked the twenty miles to and from work each day. The ride there was mostly deserted, with only five or ten houses along the entire route. I'd rarely ever see a car during the trip. The family had three kids and lived in a small dilapidated house. The house was so dirty that I'd keep the kids outside all day unless it was raining.

My dad knew that when it came to making money, I was determined. I was only twelve, and it would be four more years before I could get any real jobs. But he had already started making me buy all my own clothes and pay for more or less everything I did except eat.

My assailant was a small man, and as he faced me head on, I realized we were looking eye to eye. He pulled a small pocketknife from his pants, shifting his right leg back to brace himself as he held the knife in front of my face. Without any conscious thought to my actions, I charged into his side, sending the knife flying from his hands. In the second that it took for him to reach down and grab it, I was already running down the street as fast as I could. I knew the ride by heart, and I started visualizing the two houses that were a mile or so ahead. I never looked back as I ran faster than I ever would in my life.

My dad made me quit the babysitting job. I was too scared to bike anymore, and even too scared to go running by myself for weeks. Although I was devastated to have lost the income, it was the first time I realized how important running had become to me. Running would grow to become one of the primary influences in making me a disciplined and determined individual. Running became the therapeutic outlet I would turn to whenever I was stressed. I knew I would have to find a way to overcome my fears and return to running.

———∿∧———

"Come on Yola, walk faster and quit dragging your bag," my dad barked at me for the eighth time. "I have an exciting new adventure in store."

That's what he always said I thought. I was four, and we had been in Northern California now for 2 years. I could no longer remember Vietnam, or my mother. My dad and I were alone, forced financially to live off the land; to minimize any chance of being discovered, he had sought out an area so remote it didn't exist on a map. Redway, California, didn't have a police station. The local trade was marijuana growing.

"Where are we going this time?" I asked again, exhausted and irritated. Our first residence had been a packing crate; my dad had found the crate, dislodged from a train, abandoned on the side of the road. It provided shelter, and was better than sleeping outside. The musty smell of freight previously transported on the train would stay with me forever. I shuddered recalling the various odors. I didn't know if the train had been used to carry food or animals, but I had sniffed out every corner of the small space, and was certain it had been one of the two. The space had been four times as long as it was wide, and my dad and I had to sleep head to head. Our sleeping bags took up half the length of the crate; we lined up milk crates the rest of the length, and stored our few possessions in the containers. The interior of the crate had been too dark to do much of anything other than sleep, so we had spent pretty much all of our time hanging out outside. We found two abandoned chairs and a folding table that we set up as our dream patio.

"Enough with the questions already, I've made some friends and they are going to take us in, just be patient."

We continued walking, now up a large hill into fields that seemed to go on for miles. All I could see was grass and trees, a sea of varying shades of green. It was hot, one of the hottest days ever for Northern California. The area generally had little variability in temperature, always in the mid to high 60's, making living outside feasible. However, this particular day was in the high 80's, and I was tired from what seemed to be hours of walking. Even the leaves on the trees appeared to be sagging from the weight of the humidity in the air.

We rounded a bend after walking through a long stretch of dark forest, to finally see an opening onto a large flat field. It was probably the size of two football fields, and after the endless narrow dark stretches in the forest, it was like a hidden oasis. At first glance around the open space with overgrown brown weeds that covered my knees, I didn't see anything. But then I noticed the house; it was a very small two-story home positioned two hundred yards away in the far corner. We began walking towards it, and as the house slowly came into view, I noticed how perfect it appeared to be. Although it was very small, every feature of the house had a unique character. It was a brilliant shade of red, with black shutters on each window; the shutters appeared to be hand-carved, as I noticed the cut outs of fish and leaves within the wood. It had a wraparound porch with potted plants hanging from the many porch beams. There were stained glass chimes and two rocking chairs on either side of the front door. I looked at my dad, starting to bubble in anticipation as we continued walking toward the house.

"Is this the house we are going to live in?" I asked excitedly.

"Well, not exactly."

"What do you mean? I thought you said that we were going to live with some of your friends?"

"Well, we are, but not inside their house. You'll see, be patient. I promise you'll like it." My dad cut me off, indicating it was time to stop asking questions.

We walked up to the house and knocked on the door. A middle-aged woman in a long flowing skirt answered the door.

"Carl, so glad you made it," she said in a slow, deep voice.

I liked her instantly. There was something about her face, the way her eyes had a calming peaceful look to them; I felt comfortable around her right away.

"Yola, this is my friend Jean."

"Come in, come in," she said hurriedly, "I've made some fresh scones and you have to try them."

What's a scone, I wondered?

Scones turned out to be light, flaky pastries – I had never had a pastry before. They were delicious, made with plenty of raisins, and sprinkled with powdered sugar on top. Food was always an issue with my dad. "You eat whatever is on your plate," he would proclaim after giving me our usual rice and beans. Rice and beans, it was our daily staple: breakfast, lunch, and dinner. Occasionally, he would decide we deserved an adventurous treat. His idea of something special was often some exotic and unrecognizable meat. I'd protest, saying I was full after the serving of rice and beans, but he'd insist. "You're not going anywhere until you finish the food I've given you. Food costs money, and money is not to be wasted." One time afterwards I threw up after several bites of especially chewy and aromatic meat. He insisted for weeks it was not because of the food.

My dad grabbed my hand mid air as I reached for my third scone. "Yola, be polite, we didn't come here to eat all of Jean's food."

"Oh Carl, please, she can have as many as she wants," Jean protested.

He backed off, embarrassed to discipline me in front of anyone.

I sat and listened while Jean and my dad chatted on. My dad knew Jean from the war. He didn't know her well, but anyone who had experienced the war together formed a bond. They told stories about how they left Vietnam, who they knew who were still there, and where various people had landed. I observed that there was no mention of my mother. Jean was subtle in her questions, only clarifying that it was just the two of us, and that we were not expecting anyone else. I didn't understand our sudden departure. I didn't understand the anguish felt by a parent who loses a child. My sister was only one, and I had barely a faint memory of her existence. I didn't realize the inappropriateness of my mother's behavior. Although I cried, I didn't know it was wrong of her to lock me in a closet all day. Oddly, however, I felt no remorse at her absence. I wasn't a four-year-old child longing for the comfort of her mother.

Jean's husband came home then. Larry was a large man, very dissimilar from my short and scrawny father. I momentarily held my breath, in awe of his oversized features. Despite his appearances, he also had a soft likeable way about him. After the introductions were made, we turned to the purpose of our visit.

"Well, Carl, you are free to use any part of the back field you want to build a lean-to," Larry said. "Jean and I are honored to have you live on our land, and we will open up our house so that you can use what facilities you need."

We began work that afternoon. My dad hauled wood from Larry's woodpile, hammering the large pieces into an oak tree at an angle, building our fort against the large base of the tree. He used the smaller pieces to form panels, filling in the sides to enclose the entire structure. Jean and Larry gave us two old mattresses and some bedding to sleep on.

The first night in our incomplete lean-to was a sleepless one for both of us. Without a sealed roof, the wind whipped through my hair, making relaxing all but impossible. I tried not to complain the next morning, when we were back at work, finishing our new home, but I had tears in my eyes, trying to hold back my disappointment that we didn't get to live inside with Jean and Larry.

We finished our lean-to the second day. It was cozy inside, and Jean had given us several more items to make it home. We made a desk out of wooden crates, and a chair out of four throw pillows. We had enough blankets to cover the ground, and if you closed your eyes, you wouldn't know it was just a tree fort. I was oblivious to how unusual it was to live the way we did.

We lived in our lean-to for the next three years, and grew very close to Jean and Larry.

"Yola, come inside the house, I have a surprise for you." Jean called from her back porch one day.

I was sitting on the grass; practicing my alphabet in a new notebook my dad had just bought me. Each month when we hitchhiked into Garberville to pick up our welfare check, my dad would treat me to something special. The trip to Garberville took an hour and a half each way, and depending on how long it took before we found someone willing to pick us up, it could be an all day affair to get our money. This month I had picked out two new notebooks and several pens. I loved to draw and practice writing, and could sit for hours outside going over the same exercises.

I jumped up at the sound of Jean's voice. Jean was like a mother to me, always interested in everything I did, and every day after school I would run up to the house to show Jean what I had done in school that day. When I walked inside the house there was a multi colored patchwork dress laid out on the table.

"Is this for me? Did you make it?" I exclaimed.

"I did, I made it for you, so that you can be pretty when you go to school."

I ran to the dress, holding it up in front of the mirror. Jean had made it using many different pieces of fabric, all sewn together. There were all different colors, and all different patterns.    It was sleeveless with a big bow that tied in back. Although the various pieces were mismatched scraps of material Jean had bought from the five and dime, to me it was the most beautiful thing I'd ever seen.

I ran into her arms. "Thank you so much, I love it."

One of my dad's favorite artists was Dolly Parton.  Every time he would play her song "Coat of Many Colors," I'd dance around the house in Jean's dress. "Coat of Many Colors" became my favorite song for years to come.  Friends laughed at me in high school for knowing all the words to every song on Dolly Parton's "9-5" tape.

I couldn't wait to show my dad the dress. Jean helped me put it on, tying the bow just perfectly, and then we walked hand in hand to show my dad.

"Kiddo, wow, where did you get that fancy dress?" he proclaimed.

"Jean made it for me, just for me," I answered.

"Jean, what would we do without you? Thank you so much."

Jean went on to make me many dresses. I think she spent all her free time sewing; within a year I had six new dresses.

I hadn't had many clothes and didn't really care, until Jean started making the dresses.  There was a Salvation Army in Garberville that we would go to on welfare day occasionally. But we'd only go if one of my two outfits needed replacing. My dad wore the same pair of pants with his red and black checked shirt every day.  My clothes needed replacing more often than expected. Almost daily, I'd come home with rips and tears from trees and barbed wire fences on my daily excursions on Jean and Larry's land. My dad was good about not getting mad at me, usually stitching the rips himself. Until Jean's dresses, all my clothes had been pants and t-shirts. Now I loved dresses, and loved being proud to look like many of the other girls in my class at school. I was six now, and had just started kindergarten at a new Montessori school in the area. The owners of the school had recently completed their duty in the Peace Corps, and after stopping near Redway, fell in love with the area and decided to start a school. My dad befriended the owner, occasionally volunteering at the school, and in return I was allowed to attend at no charge. It was one of the many creative ways my dad found to give me what I needed to excel. Every minute of every day my dad spent trying to make a better life for me.

School was the first time I realized we were different. The other kids lived in real houses and had toys. The other kids talked about their favorite TV shows; we didn't have a TV. The other kids were picked up at the end of the day by their mothers in cars. My dad would walk the two miles to school to pick me up, and then we'd walk back together, on the side of the road. Jean's dresses made me feel like I fit in. I'd look forward to going to school, just to show off a new dress.

———∿∿———

"Okay kiddo, watch closely, this is how you do it." He turned the shiny rock over several times, inspecting it carefully, and holding it up for me to see how it was perfectly flat on both sides. He stretched his arm out just so, and flung the small rock out across the stream. One, two, three, four skips.

"Now my turn," I grabbed his arm, trying to get him to help me find a rock just as good.

My dad and I regularly hung out by the creek in town, passing time perfecting the art of rock skipping, and enjoying the cool breeze around the area. It was always a time for my dad to grill me on pretty much everything – from what I was learning in school, to making me recall facts from something he had recently taught me. My dad was always talking. Anywhere we went, he was always using the time as a learning opportunity. Sometimes I wished we could walk along in silence, or sit by the creek and enjoy our own thoughts. But my dad wouldn't let that happen. No matter what it was, he found something to teach me. He seemed to be an expert on every type of tree and flower that existed, and any insect or animal that would pass by. He babbled on and on incessantly, and I didn't dare tune out, because I knew it wouldn't be long before he quizzed me on something he had just said.

I was more competitive than him at rock skipping, and we could challenge each other for hours on who could get more skips.

"Here, what do you think of this one?" I reached down to grab a shiny black rock, barely thicker than a dime.

"Now that's a beauty; you have no excuse for not topping my four skips."

I smiled and pulled my arm back just as he had taught me. Slow at first, and then accelerating as I came through the swing. One, two, three. The rock disappeared after three skips; it was too small and light to make any splash at all. But it had clearly bounced only three times.

"Darnit! Not fair." I screamed, instantly turning the other way to find another rock. We wouldn't leave until I could top my dad's four skips.

My dad was pleased to see the innate competitive drive I seemed to have. He wasn't the type of dad to let me win just to boost my ego. Everything we did, we did fair and square, and I would never develop a false ego as a result. He was determined to give me everything I would need to be successful, even if our definitions of success ended up being dramatically different. My dad would tell me years later that in raising me, he saw the opportunity to recreate the childhood he was never able to have.  As I grew up and started to apply my work ethic, he vicariously lived through me, gaining an equal satisfaction in my every accomplishment.  He would tell me years later, "Yola, you were my pride and joy. You were able to do everything I was never able to do. You were my great Yola."

My dad had been used to the vagabond lifestyle for a while. After graduating college, he wasn't ready to settle down, and had volunteered for an organization called the Friends Service Society.  He was stationed in Mexico, in a remote village, and charged with helping the underprivileged improve their lives. He spent his days building homes and bridges, tutoring children, and coordinating supplies of food and clothing.  His short volunteer stint turned into a several year mission.  I never fully appreciated the work he had done in Mexico, until years later, when he returned to the villages he had worked in.  He told me stories of the parties the residents threw to welcome him back to the area.  A young boy, whom my dad had mentored, was the first boy from his village to ever attend college.  He traveled hundreds of miles to come back and thank my dad.

Landing a job at the Associated Press was an exciting moment in my dad's career.  Getting assigned to cover the Vietnam War was considered one of organization's most prestigious assignments.  He had every intention of leveraging the experience to advance his career.  He was not prepared for how much his life would change in Vietnam.  He, and all his colleagues, both reporters and soldiers, soon turned to drugs to escape the gruesome realities of the war.  Watching friends die on a daily basis was too much to bear, and almost everyone had to find a means of escape.  My dad has always had an extreme and addictive personality.  He never did anything halfway; if he took on any sort of hobby or project, he always took it to extremes, soon becoming an expert in any given area.  One year it was African art, then oriental rugs, and before long he was a world expert on calligraphy. This personality trait made him vulnerable to the addictive properties of the many drugs they were exposed to – marijuana, heroine, and opium. During the worst periods of his addiction, his entire consciousness had been consumed by where and when he would get his next fix. He would go to extreme measures to hide the drugs in various places, constantly plotting to ensure he was never without. He later told me stories of hiding small stashes in the outhouses he frequented, knowing no one would ever think to search an outhouse. During the many times he had unsuccessfully tried to quit, he would often find himself stumbling around late at night, searching outhouses for a stash he had potentially forgotten about.

As an adult, when I was addicted to Tylenol PM, he had given me advice on how to escape the addiction. "The only way to stop, kiddo, is to go cold turkey."The similarities between us were astounding. Although two Tylenol PM tablets nightly are fairly benign compared to heroin and opium, I had also been mentally consumed by the drug. If I was going to be out past 9 p.m. at night, I would hide the two little pills in a tissue and keep them in my pocket, ensuring I could take them thirty minutes before returning home, giving the medicine time to set in before bed. After 5 p.m. at night each day, I would become anxious by the approaching of the bed time hour, hoping my Tylenol PM would work to sedate me.

My insomnia and the ensuing addiction had first started six months before my marriage to Mike. It took several months for me to realize it was related to the upcoming wedding. I brushed it off as natural wedding jitters. But I knew it was more than that. I didn't feel right; I didn't feel at peace with the life I was getting myself into.

Mike and I had met at business school. In my typical hasty way, I had gotten overly involved with the first guy I met; Mike had approached me during orientation, the week before school

officially started. He was a year ahead of me, and I was flattered
to be pursued by a second year. He asked me out the third day
I landed on Duke's campus, and I was oblivious to the early
signs of his obsessive personality as he relentlessly courted me.
Almost involuntarily, I quickly lapsed into a relationship where
we spent every day together my first year of school. It was only
weeks before he had practically moved in with me.

My decision to marry Mike was made on a whim, a
personality characteristic I shared with my dad. Although I was
hesitant before the wedding, I felt obligated to go through with
it. We were married shortly after graduation, and moved to
Boston to start work. Mike worked in consulting and traveled
5 days a week. It was an easy marriage; we never saw each other.
I dove into my career, channeling all my time and energy into
work. The signs were obvious to many of our friends. I started
to travel incessantly, taking on every business trip regardless of
necessity. We almost never saw each other, and when we were
together, it was typically a social gathering.

It's hard to pinpoint exactly what made me realize it wasn't
right. There were so many warning signs – looking forward to
when he would go away Sunday night, over scheduling our little
time together to avoid being alone with him, dreading his return
Friday night. Each weekend, we would wake up early Saturday
morning to go for a one hundred mile bike ride, followed by an
eight mile run, and a mile swim. We would finish our grueling
training in the very late afternoon, with only enough time to
get ready to head out with friends. Sunday was more or less
the same routine, allowing just enough time for him to shower
and catch his flight. The few times we were alone on Saturday
nights, I found myself cringing at most of what came out of his
mouth. He loved to tell me stories of his days as a naval officer
on submarines. I wasn't the least bit impressed with the work
he had done, and consequently had little interest in his stories. I
would stare into space, mindlessly nodding at the boring details
he shared. He told me of how he had failed the entrance exam

necessary to qualify for submarines multiple times; finally, in pity, the captain had allowed him to skip the exam. These were the details I focused on; how could he not even be smart enough to pass a basic entrance exam? I had little respect for him, and although I was increasingly aware of it, I ignored it because we had fun training together. I had a passion for athletics and extreme exercise; his willingness to go along with the schedule I established was enough to justify marrying him.

I was in a rush to get married, and similar to many hasty decisions I had made in life, assumed any issues would correct themselves. I was embarrassed by my lack of respect for him, and couldn't explain it to others. Perhaps it was related to my own self-interests and obsessive competitive drive. I dismissed my irrational feelings, unwilling to slow down and think them through. Every hasty decision I had previously made had worked out; I had become overly confident in my quick decision-making, and was unable to think through future ramifications. I was always focused on the short-term, and at the present moment, I was happy enough in our relationship. I had gone to the first prestigious college that recruited me without evaluating others and everything had worked out; I took the first job offer I received after college, and had excelled in it. I had purchased the first wedding dress I tried on, and although I never loved it, it was fine. I didn't understand the potential value in slowing down and evaluating multiple options in anything, including the selection of my husband.

After 6 months I began to admit my mistake. I distanced myself further, making every effort to avoid spending time together. It took another year for me to tell Mike I didn't want to be together, and to admit my mistake to friends and family. I was most embarrassed to tell my father. His ambivalence towards Mike had been obvious. But I ignored it, too scared to ask him what he thought of Mike. He had been everything I wanted a father to be in the beginning, asking Mike about his background, his interests, and his hobbies. But after the predictable questions had been asked, there was no follow up. It was obvious he found Mike to be shallow and dull, but I wasn't willing to admit it to myself, and didn't want to hear it from my dad. I knew he would never say anything without me asking; he placed too strong of a value on independence, and he was insistent on letting me make my own mistakes. Our relationship as father and daughter had transitioned into a relationship between two adults as soon as I had started making my own money, something that happened well before I was legally an adult. As this evolution occurred, my dad had gradually stopped giving me advice on almost anything. While I would always be able to seek his opinion, it became slowly obvious that he wasn't always sharing his true feelings. It was related to the very divergent paths we chose in life, something that made him proud as a parent, but also made it more difficult for us to relate as adults.

My dad had been married to my stepmother now for fifteen years; it had been so long I almost forgot she wasn't my real mother. I had turned to calling them on the phone almost nightly. It was uncharacteristic for me; I was always too proud of my independence, and didn't want to ever lean on my parents for anything. But I craved the emotional support.

"I'm sorry kiddo. I didn't want to say anything, but I was worried you were getting into this too fast."

I wondered whether my stepmother, Pearl, also felt the same way. Pearl had been in my life since the age of ten, and knew me as well as my dad did. But she tended to go along with most of my dad's opinions.

"But why didn't you say anything?" I was surprised that he had harbored any hesitation. Carl and Pearl had been extremely excited to plan the wedding; it was representative of how my dad had always been. He was always willing to do anything and everything to give me the best he possibly could. With limited funds, they had insisted on doing everything themselves. Carl had made the invitations, using different colored wrapping paper to cut borders and create the appearance of a frame around the text. He had made all one hundred and fifty invitations by hand. He had rented books and videos from the library on flower arranging, and convinced a local farmer to let him pick all that he needed for a nominal sum. The flowers were beautiful and looked professional. Pearl had made a five-layer cake, decorated meticulously with the same flowers. She had completed four full practice runs before she was confident she could make the perfect cake on the wedding day. I never would have suspected they were anything but excited.

"It's your life, and we didn't feel it was our place to comment." He said very seriously, remorseful and apologetic of his decision.

"Well, that never stopped you before." I was half-joking, but I wondered what I would have done if my dad had told me his real thoughts. I sensed I probably would have ignored him anyway. "Can you make me a promise that next time you will tell me what you really think? You're my dad, and I care what you think." I realized I was already thinking of the next time.

"If that's what you want, that's what we'll do." He would hold his promise as he always did. My dad and I continued to talk, strategizing over ways to get out of my ugly situation with Mike. More than anything, I used him as a sounding board to voice my frustrations.

A possessive and psychotic side of Mike emerged as I began the process of ending our marriage.

"You're not leaving, I won't let you." Mike stared at me with beady determined eyes as he pinned my arms against the door. He was just over six feet tall, and athletically fit, with arms much larger and stronger than my petite frame. I wondered how I had ever thought he was remotely good looking. His thinning blonde hair and pale complexion made him look old and tired to me. His athletic build was arguably attractive, but I had already lost any sense of physical attraction towards him. It had been months since we had been intimate, and the thought of it made me cringe.

I struggled to contain my composure, scared now that he may turn violent. "Please Mike, be rational, it's just not working, you can't force it," I pleaded.

"But why? I don't understand."

We had discussed it hundreds of times; we had spent hours in marriage counseling. I had only agreed to counseling, hoping that it would help to convince him we were not right. It helped to give me the peace of mind and credible evidence I needed to feel that we had tried everything possible. The many hours of counseling had started to affect my career, making me more and more frustrated at the lack of control I felt in the situation. We had first started meeting with a counselor in Boston once a week; I snuck out of the office for two hours every Wednesday, not wanting anyone to know where I was going. But then they recommended individual counseling from a therapist in Newton; the weekly appointments required me to leave work for four hours. Before long, I was spending over $600 a week on therapy I knew was futile, all as a strategic attempt to get Mike to concede.

"I've told you over and over, I just don't love you. I'm not sure what else to say."

"But I can change, just give me a chance." He was relentless. It was difficult for me to maintain my composure, but I knew the best strategy was to remain calm.

"Please Mike, please let me leave." I cried in desperation. My wrists started to ache from the pressure of his grip as he continued to pin me against the door. He never did give in that night, and I was forced to lie next to him in bed, awake and plotting how I was ever going to escape such an awful situation.

I had turned to a bottle of wine each night as a means to escape the reality of my horrible home life. At first it was just one glass, and then two, and before I knew it, it took close to a whole bottle to ease my tensions. I started to add Tylenol PM to my regimen. The combination of the wine and the medicine was essential for me to get any sleep at all. Mike was well aware of my routine, but chose to ignore it, oblivious to how pathetic our lives had become.

I had casually mentioned the extent of my addictions to my dad, but he had maintained his style of letting me manage my problems independently. I continued to call him and report on my situation regardless, valuing his ability to listen and relate. I would never have a true understanding of what he had gone through, both in Vietnam and in California. And although he had fully recovered from every addiction he had ever faced, the personality trait would always be there, threatening his conscience when life became difficult. Even years later, when our lives were more normal, he had turned to a bottle of Guinness Stout each night to wind down; it was only several months before he was drinking a six pack every evening. He had to layer on a glass of orange juice and vodka to maintain the same effect. Similar to the heroin and opium, he eventually quit the Guinness and vodka cold turkey, but not without hours of mental anguish and failed attempts.

The next day I left work early, entering our apartment when I was sure he would not be there. I packed just my clothes; hesitant to take only possessions he couldn't claim as joint. Our realtor had found me a month-to-month furnished apartment in a nearby doorman building. I left Mike a note, explaining that he had left me with no choice. I felt momentary comfort that I at least now had a place of my own. I naively assumed he wouldn't be able to find me in the small city of Boston. After dropping my stuff off at my new home, I walked to the meeting I had arranged with a divorce attorney.

"Tell me about yourself. Tell me about your marriage and why you would like a divorce."

Ailsa wanted to know my whole background, wanted to understand my rationale for giving up and seeking divorce. I struggled to explain it in coherent terms. Mike had never beaten me, had never cheated on me, had really never done anything other than be loyal and reliable. On the surface we got along well and shared many similarities. We enjoyed challenging each other to marathons and triathlons. Our abilities were similarly matched. The only time we spent together was consumed with exercising. We were successful business school grads. On paper we sounded perfect.

"There's no passion," I tried to explain. "We don't have real conversations, I don't respect him."

Even my lawyer didn't understand, I could tell. But it wasn't her job to understand, it was her job to help me complete the divorce process. Fortunately, Mike's recent slightly violent and irrational behavior gave her urgency in wanting to help me. I left her office with the semblance of a plan. She estimated it would take at least a year before I could call myself a single woman again.

I awoke early the next day, having barely slept after my first night in a strange apartment. I put on my running clothes, eager to get outside and wake up with a 6-mile run along the river. I couldn't believe it as I exited the building; Mike was sitting on the front steps, also in his running clothes.

"Hi Hon, I thought I'd join you." He said it so casually I almost laughed. It was as though we were friends who had agreed to a 6 am run, rather than estranged husband and wife.

"How did you find me? What are you doing here?" I stammered. I struggled to look into his beady eyes. I couldn't remember what about him I was initially attracted to. I now hated him so much that he only looked hideous and possessed to me.

I had specifically told our realtor that I was looking for an obscure apartment building where Mike couldn't find me. I figured Mike would assume I was staying with friends.

"Oh, Rene told me." Rene was the realtor. How could Rene break his promise to me? I couldn't believe it. I tried to dodge him, still attempting to get in my run. He quickly strode in next to me. I ran faster, although knowing there was no way to out run him. We were too equally matched. I refused to say a word as he chatted on incessantly with casual small talk.

I called Rene's office, barely able to speak, I was so angry. It turned out his assistant, not knowing the situation, had told Mike of my whereabouts. I insisted to Rene he had to break the lease and find me a new place to live instantly. I again left work early the next day, moving several blocks away to a new apartment building. I again felt a naïve sense of comfort in my new surroundings.

Weeks went by, and I relaxed, more confident that I had now dodged him. The divorce proceedings were beginning, and I was seeing him at our weekly negotiation meetings.

"Yolanda makes well more than 50% of the couple's income, and has additionally paid off all of the couple's student loans, but she is willing to go 50/50 on the assets." My lawyer addressed Mike's lawyer as the two of us sat next to them, glaring at each other from across the table.

It was emotionally draining to endure, but my hatred towards him had only built over the last several months. All I wanted was to never see him again. I wanted to escape. I had even interviewed at a company in California, thinking it would be easier to get as far away from him as possible. But leaving the Northeast would mean leaving my family and my friends. One friend in particular had become especially important to me. It would be letting Mike get the best of me, and I knew I couldn't let it go that far.

How could I make a mistake so significant? How could I willingly follow through with a marriage when I sensed that something was wrong?

# Chapter 2 – Money obsessions

My obsession with money started at a young age, as soon as I realized others had more than us. We went to the Laundromat in Redway weekly, one of my favorite activities. The town of Redway encompassed four blocks along one narrow road. The road was lined with grubby storefronts: Patty's breakfast café, The Village Bookstore, Mike's knickknacks. The signs on most stores were in much need of repair, with Patty's hanging at a slight angle after one storm knocked the screw off the right side. The Laundromat was located just on the edge of the town, across a busy street, and next to a vacant parking lot. The structure looked barely supported by two faded red beams, with an unpainted concrete porch, and a faded old red sign that read, "Redway Laundromat." There was only one Laundromat in town, and at rush hour could have a forty-five minute wait for a washer. The dust from the abandoned dirt parking lot was always blowing outside, and the door to the Laundromat had to always be kept closed to keep the clothes clean. I loved the smell of the powdered detergent, and would breathe in deeply every time someone would crack open one of the sample-sized boxes of Tide that came out of the dispensing machine.

While my dad read his book outside, sitting with his

pipe on the curb, I would get down on my hands and knees, searching under all the washers and dryers for dropped coins. I was occasionally lucky enough to find coins left right in the dispensers. The area under the detergent dispenser was a goldmine. Each trip to the Laundromat was usually worth at least two quarters. I knew the larger coins were quarters and they were worth more. My dad knew what I was doing, but he left me to my activity, never asking for the money, or inquiring how much I had found.

"Hey, what are you doing?" A boy my age said to me as I leaned as far as I could under a dryer to try to reach a quarter.

No one had ever spoken to me before, and I was startled by the interruption, but also proud to brag of my winnings. "I just found a quarter, and I'm going to go down to Richards and buy a piece of chocolate with it."

"That's not your money," he scolded me, "you should return it to the front counter."

"It is too my money, I found it."

We went back and forth for ten minutes, and then Sammy said he had an idea. He had a ruler at home, and thought that if we got the ruler, we might be able to reach some of the coins that I could never quite get with my hands. I had long skinny arms and was both underweight and agile, but there were always coins well out of my reach no matter how hard I tried.

We walked to Sammy's house, several steps away from the Laundromat. My dad didn't seem to mind, as he was thoroughly engrossed in his book, a position he was likely to be in for most of any given day. I couldn't believe it when I saw Sammy's house. I had no concept of what toys were; Sammy's whole room was filled with toys. Model trucks, puzzles, stuffed animals. Even a whole bookshelf filled with many of my favorite books. We went to the library in town almost every day. I didn't realize people bought books for themselves and kept bookshelves full of them at home.

Sammy and I retrieved the ruler and went back to find

another three quarters that day.  Every time I'd go to the Laundromat I'd look around, hoping to see Sammy outside, and every time he'd invite me over. We'd play with some of his toys, and then go back to the Laundromat to retrieve more money with his ruler; we'd then sit outside, dividing our winnings for the day.

"One for you, one for me," I counted out the eight quarters we had found that day.

Sammy and I walked back to his house to meet up with some of the other neighborhood children. One of our regular activities was challenging the kids on the block to running races for money. I was the fastest, and no one had yet beaten me. Between the Laundromat and my races I was able to buy an ice cream at Rockies almost every day. I didn't tell my dad. Sammy knew I was fast too, so for a commission, he'd rally up friends on the street to take me on.  One day I ran races against 15 different kids. I beat them all, one after the other, and filled my coin jar. I had started filling empty baked bean cans with my coins, and lined them up in our lean-to. I enjoyed watching each can fill up, dreaming of what I would do with all the money I was collecting. Even years later I would casually take quarters from my dad's coin basket. I naively assumed he never noticed, and would line up the coins along the floorboard in my room, trying to get enough to circle the entire room.  My obsession with money continued for years and years.

Similar to the Laundromat, my dad knew what I was doing, but didn't say anything, or ask how much money I had made. He'd just sigh at how dirty I was.

"Kiddo, where have you been?"  He barked at me as I walked back to the Laundromat. "Our clothes have been ready for 10 minutes, and I've been waiting for you."

"I've been running races, and Sammy found two more kids to challenge me." I answered.

"Well, did you at least show them who's the fastest?"  I couldn't tell if he was smiling or not.

"I did, no one has beaten me yet."

He was proud. I was excelling at school, and although I was not paying the tuition everyone else was, the teacher had taken an interest in me. Now he could brag to all his friends that I was also a fast runner. "Try not to be late again." He said in his stern fatherly way.

My dad is a true intellectual; every hobby he takes on is for the true intellectual pursuit, regardless of whether or not he could make a living with his interests. I was the complete opposite; my interests always revolved around making money. Perhaps my dad left me alone to collect coins from the Laundromat floor and challenge kids to running races because he couldn't identify with my early obsessions. As much as I was a product of my dad, with many shared personality traits, one identifying characteristic that he didn't share at all was my intense focus on money and career success.

My dad spent all his time working to educate me, instilling in me values of hard work and discipline. Our definition of success was noticeably different as soon as I had an understanding of money, which was at a surprisingly young age. My dad would always be there to challenge and teach me, but we had an unspoken difference in what we chose to do with our pursuits and knowledge.

It was welfare day. Every month, on the second or third day of the month, my dad and I would go to Garberville to pick up our welfare check. I learned the months of the year at a very young age, because my dad would always announce when it was a new month, and we'd get excited for the trip to Garberville.

My dad never seemed ashamed of our situation. Each new month, we would grow equally excited for the infusion of cash that would land in my dad's pocket. To this day, he has never been a good manager of money, and we would invariably spend too much of our month's allotment on the first day. My dad had grown up in a middle class household, with a father who was probably a step above my dad in his intellectual interests. But his father's intellectual pursuits had taken away from his time and abilities in being a father. My dad had grown up feeling bitterness towards his own father. Although my grandfather was responsible for several inventions and had won numerous awards in science, my father had little respect for him. "He's a bitter man," was all my dad would say when I asked him about his father. Carl grew up confused by what he saw as a trade off between career success and family. His own father had achieved career success, but completely failed in his devotion to his family. Although our lives were far from normal, and we were surviving off the government, my dad was determined to do a better job than his father had in raising his only child. His extreme personality didn't allow him, at least for a while, to find a balance between work and family; he chose to spend all his time trying to be a good dad. I would later face a similar struggle, a challenge that led me to relive my childhood and reflect on my dad's dilemma. Our extreme and obsessive personalities didn't allow us to do anything less than 100%.

Garberville was more than sixty miles south of Redway, along narrow roads lined with towering Redwood trees. The ride took more than an hour and a half. Redway was known for its historic trees, many rising more than one hundred feet in the air. The awesome forests were hundreds of years old, and the trees had trunks wider around than a giant cement mixer. Many had fallen over during bad storms, and it was a challenging climb to get on top of a trunk and lean over to count the rings. I would often try to count the concentric circles on some of the older fallen down trunks, but would lose track after two hundred or so. Driving down the narrow roads densely lined with the Redway trees was a brilliant sight. All you could see for miles and miles was one tree trunk after another, all coated in thick green leaves. The aroma was so powerful you could still smell it even with closed windows.

Since we didn't have a car, and there was no public transportation, the only way to Garberville was to hitchhike.

"Okay kiddo, now remember everything I've taught you about how to stand, and how to hold out your thumb. I'll go stand on the other side of the street."

My dad has a specific strategy for how best to hitchhike. He had pounded into me the associated risks, and claimed that if we used his method, we would always be safe. His strategy involved us splitting up; he would stand on one side of the street, and me on the other. He would stand further up in the direction the cars were traveling, so he could get the first look. If a car and its driver looked safe, he'd give me the signal, a tap of his foot, and I'd stick out my thumb, smiling just so. I was to look friendly, but not overly naive or desperate. It was a smile that took months to perfect. "No, not that way, curl your lips more," my dad would say.

Although the process to learn how to hitchhike correctly was exhausting, I loved welfare day. It was an adventure, and I usually got to leave school early, so we had enough time to get to Garberville and back before dark. It was a special treat to see my dad at school, arriving in his red and black checked shirt that he wore daily. It made me feel special; not different like I always felt at school, but like I was the lucky one that day. I never told anyone at school why we left early once a month; I didn't care what they thought this time.

The welfare check was always the only thing in our PO Box. Although it was our only mailbox, there was never anything else. We didn't have any bills, and pretty much no one knew where we were. We weren't on any catalogue mailing lists, because we had never purchased anything.

I jumped to attention, seeing my dad tap his foot, indicating the oncoming car was safe to solicit a ride from. I quickly stepped forward, slightly into the street, but not so much as to get hurt, and thrust my thumb out while smiling casually. No luck, the green Chevrolet continued along without decelerating; I wasn't even sure the driver had seen my thumb.

"Better luck next time," my dad screamed from across the street, "try to move a little more quickly when you see me tap my foot. You were daydreaming."

I looked down at my feet, upset that I had disappointed my dad. I didn't want him to see that I was upset; I knew he'd only ridicule me for not being tough enough. I was barely old enough to walk down a street on my own, and my dad already had me jumping into streets to flag down car rides. I thought nothing of how inappropriate this was, and for my dad, there was nothing unusual about it at all. We were a father and daughter team, and although I was only five years old, I had to share equally in our life responsibilities. I didn't appreciate that this was actually more challenging as a parent. It's often easier to coddle and protect your children than it is to push independence and work on them. A child's natural tendency is to want to be taken care of; it takes strength as a parent to ease your kid into eventually taking care of themselves.

"Got it," I screamed from across the street.

I stood there for another fifteen minutes, waiting for my dad to tap his foot, but he let car after car pass by. They all looked pretty much fine to me. But I didn't dare doubt whatever concerns he had. Finally, another foot tap. I jumped into action as quick as I could, moving farther into the street, to make sure the driver saw me this time. It worked. The rusted blue pick up truck slowed down as it approached, an elderly man wearing a cowboy hat leaning out the window.

"Can I help ya little girl?" He pushed aside his chewing tobacco.

I wondered what my dad saw in this particular car and driver; so many nicer looking cars had sped by unapproved by my dad.

"Yes sir, my dad and I are headed to Garberville." I indicated across the street to my dad.

"Hop on in; so am I." He smiled meekly, and leaned across to open the passenger door.

My dad walked across the street to grab my hand, and we piled into the cramped small cabin of the truck. It was too long of a drive for us to sit in the back, but the front barely had enough room for two people. I sat on my dad's lap.

We made it safely to Garberville, all for what would be two quick stops – one at the post office and one at the bakery. We'd then spend another hour trying to find a ride back. It usually took a little less time leaving Garberville since there were many more cars, but it was often difficult to find someone going as far north as Redway. We often had to hitchhike two separate times to get home. It was especially tough if we made it home much after dark, since the walk from the road to our lean-to was unlit, and coated with loose rocks and fallen down branches. It was impossible not to trip in the dark.

~~~

My dad had quickly made friends in Redway. It was a slow moving town, with people generally not up to much. Many residents didn't seem to work at all. I found out years later it was because the main trade was marijuana growing. Most people grew some amount of marijuana in their homes, and survived financially from the proceeds. Even though you could smell the very distinguishable smell emanating out of many houses throughout the day, no one thought anything of it.

My dad contemplated joining in the trade. It would give us supplemental money, and allow my dad to buy many of the things he wished I could have. It was a constant guilt he had. In Vietnam, although our lives were in shambles from my parent's disastrous relationship, we at least had a nice apartment, as well as a maid, and had been able to purchase material things. My dad was a graduate of Tufts University and The New School of Research. Both were well-respected institutions; the odds of a graduate ending up homeless were considered near zero. My dad rationalized that he had no choice; there had been no other way to escape and ensure my safety. He only wished there was another alternative, but there was none he could think of. His moral conscience wouldn't allow him to expose me to the life of a marijuana grower. Even though I was too young to understand, he knew it was not something he himself would be proud of. He felt he had already made too many mistakes, and now as a single parent, he had every opportunity to make up for his errors of judgment. He had the chance to raise a successful child. He realized the cynicism he exhibited in still using marijuana, but his use was relatively infrequent, and he knew he could cut the occasional habit cold turkey if he wanted to. He was not as confident he could grow accustomed to the income from selling, and give that up as quickly.

One of his best friends was a character that I instantly fell in love with. Paco was the local auto mechanic, operating "Paco's Garage" in the center of town. We'd often walk over to Paco's, and hang out, watching clients pull up to get their cars fixed. Even though Paco owned the shop, it was mostly his workers who would do the actual work, and Paco spent a lot of time on his music. He was Spanish, and had an addictive and melodic voice. I could spend hours sitting in front of him while he played his guitar and sang his songs. Even though he repeated many of the same songs over and over, I didn't care. I'd get lost in the words I didn't even understand, and often drift off into my daydreams of a better life.

My teeth had recently started to cause me a lot of embarrassment at school, and I would do anything to get away from places where I had to deal with people staring at my teeth. My teeth had come in without enamel, and every single tooth was a horrific shade of brown and yellow. I worked hard to learn how to not open my mouth too wide, and modified my smile to be a closed lip grin. Whenever I spoke at school or in front of strangers, I could sense people staring into my mouth, and I hated it. Paco would sing songs about beautiful Spanish women and love, and I'd daydream, pretending I was also beautiful, despite my ugly teeth.

My dad was worried about my teeth as well, and had even shelled out the money to take me to the dentist. There was nothing the dentist could do, short of putting fakes in place of all my baby teeth. It was prohibitively expensive, and they were only baby teeth anyway. He told my dad he had no idea if my permanent teeth would also come in without enamel, but assumed it was likely they would.

My dad took very few pictures during our time in California, but one that I would always remember was a picture of me sitting on the steps in town, holding my Raggedy Ann doll and smiling my brown smile.

We spent the night at Paco's place that night, and I drifted off to sleep, smelling the heavy aroma of marijuana and listening to my dad and Paco roar with laughter as they stayed up all night telling stories. They would smoke so much pot together that the stimulating effects would keep them up straight through the night.

My dad surprised me with a gift one day – a journal. "Kiddo, I thought you'd enjoy using this as a diary," he said very seriously. "Keeping a diary takes a lot of discipline, and I think it would be a nice challenge for you to write in it everyday."

He always spoke of everything as challenges. "What challenge can we tackle this week?" he would say. I came to love my diary. Every night before going to bed, I'd look forward to writing in it. Sometimes I'd write two or three pages, going over everything I had done that day. It was fun to read over past pages, reliving each day and each experience. *"We hung out at Paco's garage today. It never seems like anyone comes to the garage. All Paco does is sit on the steps and play his guitar. Today he played my favorite song. I can't remember the name of it, but it's about a famous girl. Maybe one day I can grow up to be like the girl in his song."* At the end of each page I'd always finish with the same thing.

"Someday I'm going to grow up and be rich," I would write. I never showed this to my dad, but I was determined. I was six years old, and I was determined that when I grew up I was going to make a lot of money. I had little understanding of what was necessary to do so, or of the pros and cons of having money. All I knew was that we had very little money, and that was why we didn't live in a normal house, why I had no toys, and why we had to eat rice and beans everyday. Each day I would fill a page in my diary with dreams. After writing my thoughts about each day, I'd close my eyes and imagine myself in the future. I'd imagine a large house, a refrigerator filled with every food imaginable, a library stocked with shelves and shelves of books. My dad was always in my dreams; I longed for both my dad and I to have many of the things I'd see my classmates with. My dad always drove a fancy car in my dreams, with me in the backseat dressed in a brand new outfit.

My dad was impressed with my diligence in writing in my diary. Although he never asked to read any of it, he would watch proudly from afar as I spent hours with my pen. As a journalist, he assumed the time was good practice on my writing skills. As our different pursuits and definitions of success became apparent over time, my dad would have probably struggled to rationalize most of what I was writing. My diary was my first use of writing as a therapeutic outlet. I would later use letters to express my feelings in any relationship I was involved in, including deeper issues my dad and I would eventually face. I would always love writing, just as my dad did, but even my dad had steered me away from a career in writing when I ventured out into the work force. As much as our pursuits of money were different, he understood my motivations and guided me appropriately.

—◊—

I went to business school for one reason: to get a job at Freedom.

I knew I wanted to manage money, and I only wanted to do it at the best mutual fund company there was. My classmates laughed at me when I started my job search the second week of school. The first week of school I spent securing a part time job at a local mutual fund. I told them I'd do anything. I just needed a job in the industry on my resume. I spent ten hours a week researching companies for them. I called the human resources rep at Freedom every day for three weeks.

"We don't recruit at Fuqua, but you're welcome to send in your resume," she said.

I didn't hear back so I called her again.

Finally, irritated, she responded to me, "I guess if you're ever in Boston you can stop by and we'll have someone interview you."

I lied. "I'll be in Boston all next week, would there be anyone available then?"

I'd irritated her so much she gave me an interview just to get rid of me. I blew $800 on the trip back and forth to Boston, money I didn't have. But I knew I had to give myself the chance.

Kevin was my first interview.

"I know you're smart. Tell me something more interesting." He quickly scanned down my resume, turning it over onto his desk.

Great, I thought. He appeared completely disinterested.

"Umm, I compete in triathlons." I muttered, not knowing what to say."

"What distances? I'm a triathlete." His eyes lit up, and he stopped flipping his pen back and forth between his fingers.

We ended up hitting it off right away. Kevin was thoroughly impressed that I had done distances as long as half-ironmans. My times were even better than his.

I got the internship before Freedom even started their on-campus interviewing. My dad was my first call. "You're going to do it kiddo, you're going to make millions." My dad had laughed at my dreams as a kid, but regardless of my pursuit, he was my biggest fan. His words meant the world to me.

———ᴧᴧ~

"What are you doing?" Craig asked, peering into my office.

Craig and I were summer interns at Freedom together. We had eight interns in our class. They told us that everyone good could get a job, but the competition was fierce, and we all knew that we had to get our stocks right, communicate our views succinctly, and work harder than anyone else. I was logging seven days a week, staying until ten at night most days. They had assigned me eleven stocks. They were all mine. I was expected to decide whether each was a buy or a sell, and convince the forty odd portfolio managers to listen to my views. I was responsible for these stocks across the entire five hundred billion dollars of equity money managed in our department.

"I can't take it, Daisy Tech is down another quarter point today, I had to cover my screen."

I had taped a piece of paper over my quote machine. It was impossible to not occasionally lift it to see the latest stock prices, but at least if it was covered, I avoided the constant urge to simply stare at the screen and try to will the stocks I had rated buys to go up. Daisy Tech was one of my eleven companies. I had just rated it a buy and had even convinced the manager of the Money Fund, Freedom's largest fund, to buy it. I couldn't believe it when I walked into his office. I was just out of business school, barely understood what made stocks work, and on five minutes of explaining why I liked Daisy Tech, he bought it, just like that. And he didn't buy a small position - he bought one million shares of it. I sweated in excitement, and then my excitement quickly turned to fear. Daisy Tech had to go up.

"Calm down," Craig said, "you just put a buy on it two days ago, give it time."

"Yeah, but Bob bought it," I argued, "if it doesn't go up I'll never get the job, he'll think I'm an idiot."

"Well, you should walk around then."

"Walking around." That was supposedly the most important aspect to getting the job. Walking around meant walking the halls, looking for portfolio managers to speak with. Most of the portfolio managers traveled two to three days a week. Even when they were in the office, they were typically in company meetings. If they actually happened to be at their desk, they were most likely on the phone. So walking around generally entailed standing outside of a portfolio manager's office, hoping and waiting for them to get off the phone. It was easy to burn an hour roaming the halls without ever talking to anyone. When you actually got the chance to talk to a portfolio manager there was no question who was the more senior person in the room. Most of the portfolio managers used the opportunity when you were talking to open their mail, file, or input data into their computer. Rarely did you have the opportunity to have a real conversation, one where two people exchanged dialogue and maintained eye contact at the same time.

Off I went. Craig was right – I had to walk the halls. If all my stock picks were wrong, maybe I could save myself with my engaging personality, or sheer will to walk the floors all day. I tried to spend from nine a.m. to five p.m. everyday doing the walk. The odds of catching people during the busiest hours were highest, and that left the evening to do the actual work.

I knocked. He still didn't look up. Should I knock again? I decided to do it. Finally, a single eye peered from behind a research report. "Hi, I'm Yolanda, I'm one of the summer interns." I tried to sound cheery. He looked back down at his reading and ignored me. Okay, now what do I do? Should I knock again? Should I talk anyway? I decided to go for the latter. "I'm recommending Daisy Tech, and I was hoping to tell you about it," I ventured. Still no response. "Ummm, I think it has fifty percent upside. They're revamping all their factories, and they think they can increase margins by five percent over two years."

Finally, my words seemed to register. He put down the research report, stood up from behind his desk, and came over to my side.

"I don't buy small cap stocks. I manage the large cap value fund, please don't pitch me on small cap stocks again." With that he sat back down in his chair and resumed reading the research report.

"Uh, sorry." I stammered as I backed out of his office. Great, that exchange was unlikely to get me the full-time job.

I knocked again. I had to walk by three occupied offices before I finally regained the courage to try to talk with another portfolio manager. "Hi, can I help you." Finally, a friendly voice.

"Hi, I'm Yolanda, and I'm one of the summer interns. I was hoping to pitch you on Daisy Tek."

"Sure, what do ya got?" He asked in a friendly voice, putting me at ease.

"Come on in." He signaled for me to take a seat. A seat, wow, I never imagined actually sitting down in a portfolio manger's office. I figured I should take the seat, for fear of looking rude.

"Well, they're revamping their factories and expect to increase margins by five percent over two yeas." I started into my pitch.

I was quickly interrupted. "What are the incremental margins? How do you validate the five percent?"

Incremental margins. I tried to visualize my accounting book. Gross margins, pre-tax margins, net margins. There were many kinds of margins, but I didn't remember learning about incremental margins.

"Umm, well the gross margins are estimated at 21.5% for next year, up from 17% last year." I figured that would be a good enough answer.

"Do you know what I'm asking? What percent of the costs are fixed? What percent of the costs are variable?" He started talking and asking questions faster than I could follow.

"Um, I'm not sure."

"Well, let's think about it." "If the factory is already up and running, how much do you think it costs to make one extra unit?"

"Ummm, I don't know." The conversation went on and on. My only answer was "I don't know." I must have said, "I don't know" thirty times.

Two hours later, six conversations later, I was convinced that I had officially blown it. I was never going to get the job. One portfolio manager had even slammed the door in my face, telling me to come back when I really understood my companies. I walked slowly back to my office, hoping to at least commiserate with my fellow summer interns. Even though we were all competing with each other, we were in it together, and were quickly becoming good friends. My reaction to the animosity was to hide under my desk. Craig's reaction was to throw things in his office. He broke his phone the second week on the job. Doug's reaction was to go out drinking.

"Hey, it's me Carl."

"Hey Kiddo, where are you?"

I called my dad almost every time I traveled.

"I'm at the Ritz Carlton in Chicago. Right now I'm on the roof deck, sitting by the pool doing work."

"Are you kidding? You've got the life."

I loved to share everything with my dad. He still wanted to know all my flight information, and was even doing his own research on the companies I covered so that he could ask intelligent questions.

"I've got my industry review next week. This is it, this will be the make it or break it on whether or not I get the job."

"You'll do it, I know you will, we're rooting for you." My dad's praise had come and gone over the years; for now, it seemed to be all praise and confidence. The unpredictable reactions I received from my dad occasionally caused me frustration, but I was so focused on pleasing him that I usually thought nothing of it. I had entered a new stage of my life, one where my interests and lifestyle had progressively moved farther and farther away from my upbringing. As much as I loved and respected my dad, I was still at a point in my life where I was striving to move beyond my childhood. It would be years before I was able to look back on my childhood and feel proud of what we had overcome. I eventually started to realize that my dad's feedback was related to what the topic was – if it was an area he was an expert in, he chose to challenge me by criticizing anything but perfection; as I moved farther into the world of finance and away from his knowledge base, he was more likely to praise any of my accomplishments. In school, nothing but an A+ was good enough; he had been a good student himself, and he felt confidence in pushing me to perfection. When it came to my running, an area where he lacked any abilities, he was more willing to reward my every achievement. I would later struggle with what is the best means of motivating someone. Many people respond positively to praise, wanting to do better and better as a result. Others need criticism and the extra push to be motivated. Everyone is different, and my dad, in his effort to be the best father he could be, was attempting to adapt to each situation, choosing his reactions carefully.

---

I had to take one last trip to New York City – the last business trip I would make before presenting my industry review. I was sad to see the summer coming to an end, knowing there was a distinct possibility I wouldn't be offered the full-time job at Freedom. I loved the travel; I loved sitting in the mahogany conference rooms in the plush leather chairs, interviewing company management teams as though I was the most important person in the world. One CEO's office had been on an unmarked floor. To access the floor, an armed guard had taken me down a corridor hidden behind a secret door. From there he used a special key to access the hidden elevator. The floor was the epitome of corporate excess; the floors were covered in antique rugs, with every space on the wall occupied by beautiful art work, including pieces by artists I recognized – original Renoirs and one by Degas. I struggled to act casual, not wanting to give away my youth and naiveté. The management teams were used to the Freedom system. They knew Freedom used its analyst program as training ground for diversified portfolio managers; they knew that analysts rotated groups ever eighteen to twenty-four months. Some of the largest corporations in the country, and their associated management teams, had to cater to young, straight out of business school Freedom interns, eager to get an edge and secure the full-time job. Consequently, we all badgered the CEO's, CFO's, and COO's beyond the point of politeness, asking each question over and over with a different angle. "I know you said you couldn't disclose the margins in that business line, but let's think about it this way…"

I was at the headquarters of one of the largest banks in the country. I had set up the meetings in an effort to get any last shred of unique information to impress the audience during my industry review. I was exhausted from staying up most of the previous night preparing for the meetings, and couldn't wait to go back to the hotel room and go for a run in Central Park. One of my favorite things about traveling was the opportunity to run in different cities. I had spent several years living in New York City after undergraduate school, and missed running in Central Park. I still knew the 6.2 mile loop around the park perfectly; I would always look forward to the one hill that started around 100th street; it went on for close to a mile, and gradually increased in slope. I would always see joggers crap out on this hill, stopping to walk or stretch. That was how I knew they were joggers; no runners would stop to walk. I would often count people I passed to make the run go by quickly, and to give myself a goal. Each time I'd do the loop, I'd try to pass more runners than I had the previous time.

I quickly changed out of my business clothes, putting on running shorts and a tank top. It was hot, and if it weren't for the fact that I was in New York City, where passer bys weren't shy to whistle, I would have worn only a jogging bra. I was staying at The Penninsula Hotel; the spot that had quickly become my favorite in the city. The beds were incredibly soft, with layers and layers of down comforters. The light system was high tech, allowing you to activate any light in the room from the phone base. My favorite part was the television built into the wall beside the bathtub. I would always take a bath at night, using all the free toiletries the hotel provided. After my bath, I'd indulge in room service, ordering a sampling of many of the items off the menu. Freedom didn't have much of a policy associated with business expenses, and I knew many analysts and fund managers would stay in even more expensive hotels and treat friends to fancy restaurants. I always preferred room service, and the feeling of luxury by spending the evening in the hotel room. It allowed me to continue working through the night. But before I could enjoy the room, I had to get in my daily run. It was already 6 p.m, and was quite dark.

I almost tripped down the stairs as I went to exit the hotel. I tried to look the other way, pretending I hadn't noticed him, but there was no way to avoid him. He was literally sitting right in the middle of the hotel steps.

"Mike, what are you doing here?" My voice wavered; seeing him in New York City, where I had felt safe and away from him, made me now truly scared. How did he know I was on a business trip in New York City? Who could have told him?

"I want to talk. Please, can we just talk things through? Here, look at this." He handed me a picture of the two of us together from business school. We were standing in front of the local Chinese restaurant where we would go for dinner several times a week. He was holding his arms up in a goofy manner, making the symbol for a touchdown. We looked happy. But even at that moment, I remembered being curious as to how I truly felt about him. Several times he had come over to my apartment at business school, and I had pretended to be asleep, letting him ring the doorbell over and over. I thought nothing of how odd that was when it was time to get married.

# Chapter 3 – Male figures

I grew to love my school despite being picked on by the wealthier kids. I had made several friends, enough to make me not care about being in the unpopular crowd. I loved the different workstations, and was excited each day to see what projects would be set up. The school was run in typical Montessori fashion, with little teacher guidance and minimal structure. Each kid was left to work on whatever project most interested them, and I would spend most of my day doing the science experiments. I loved the preciseness that was required in measuring and mixing, and the suspense of not knowing what you were going to create.

The special attention I received from the teacher was noticeable to everyone. I wasn't sure if it was because I was attending the school at no charge, or because he had a genuine fondness for me, but Mr. Quinn would go out of his way to tell me how smart I was each day. "You are going to do big things Yola," he would always say. Hearing his words made me even more motivated; I constantly strived to impress him and please him. Whenever there were things to be set up or cleaned up in the classroom, I was always the first to volunteer.

The school was down a long dirt road, back sufficiently far

that you would never see it if you didn't know where it was. There were two buildings – one in front for the older children, and one in back for the younger children. A large Mulberry pole was set up between the two buildings, with streams of colorful scarves for the daily game of dancing around the Mulberry pole. I loved recess time, when we would get to run free around the large property of the school and play the game. Even though it was pure chance, I was always determined to win. I loved being number one at anything, and if the teacher had let me, I would have challenged the other kids to running races.

"Mr. Quinn, Yola is cheating!" Sandra, a snobby well-dressed girl, who I couldn't stand, was always finding ways to get me in trouble.

"What happened ladies?" Mr. Quinn was incessantly calm, no matter the circumstance. He spoke slowly and precisely, never anxious, even when our cat fights sometimes got vicious.

"She's running too fast around the Mulberry pole, and the rest of us can't get a chance." She was constantly whining, complaining that she couldn't keep up.

"That's ridiculous," I retorted, sounding like an adult with my choice of words.

"Anyway, she smells, and her teeth are brown and yucky." With that, Sandra's cohort surrounded her – four other snobby and well-dressed girls that were known to do play dates together every afternoon.

"Yeah, she smells." They all chimed in.

I turned and walked back inside the classroom, keeping my head low so I didn't have to make eye contact with anyone. Almost daily, Sandra, or someone from her clique, would make something up to get me in trouble, and end up picking on my odor, clothes, or brown teeth. I held back tears; there was no way they were going to see me cry.

"Hey Yola, I'm sorry about that." Mr. Quinn had followed me inside, where I had attempted to hide in the back science area. "Those girls are just jealous of you. They're jealous because you're smarter than them and a faster runner than they are." Mr. Quinn went on again to tell me how talented I was, but I didn't feel like hearing it. I was tired of being picked on, and tired of being different.

My friend Jason came in from outside, and gave me a friendly whack on the back. "I can't stand those girls either, don't let them get you down Yola."

Jason's words made me feel better, and I promised both he and Mr. Quinn I wouldn't let them get the best of me.

"After school, do you want to come over to my house and watch TV?" Jason asked.

I had been curious about TV and hadn't yet been to Jason's house, so I quickly took him up on his offer.

"Sure, after my dad picks me up, I'll ask him if we can walk by your house on the way home."

My dad was eager for me to make friends, and readily agreed to the visit. Jason's house was overflowing with furniture, knick-knacks, and clothes, everything you could think of. It was the messiest house I'd ever seen. I was more fascinated with inspecting everything that was in the house than I was interested in watching TV.

"Wow, you guys sure do have a lot of stuff," I commented.

"Yeah, my mom likes to go to garage sales and flea markets. She comes home with car loads full of stuff every weekend, and then she resells everything at other flea markets." Jason explained. "Who knows if she makes any money doing it, but she's always bragging about some item she bought and ended up selling for ten times what she paid."

There were shelves full of every porcelain item you could imagine. A porcelain cat, porcelain elephant, stacks of vases in different colors and shapes. In the corner was a huge pile of clothes, bags, and shoes in varying colors and sizes. On one of the tables were candy bowls and cookie jars. Most of the candy bowls were filled; one bowl had jellybeans, another was overflowing with M&M's.

"Is it okay if I help myself to some of the candy?" I asked Jason. "Sure, help yourself. There's no telling how old some of it is, but I guess candy doesn't matter."

My dad never allowed candy or anything sweet for that matter, so I was eager to sample everything.

We watched a couple of TV shows for the next hour.

"Honest, you've never seen TV before?" Jason was shocked when I didn't know any of the shows he liked.

"No, my dad doesn't believe in it. Besides, TV's are expensive I think, and we can't afford it."

"Yeah, but it's a TV, everyone has a TV.

Everyone else seemed to have everything. The other kids at school showed up with their fancy lunchboxes; my lunch was a peanut butter and jelly sandwich in a brown paper bag; it was always the same thing. I'd look around, watching in jealousy as each kid excitedly opened their box, curious as to what treats their moms had packed them that day. Each was filled with an assortment of items – a main course, a fruit, a juice box, and a treat. I never got a treat. Everyone else had a car; it seemed to be a basic life necessity, but not for us. Everyone else lived in real houses and didn't have to care what the weather was going to be on a given day. When it rained, the floor in our lean-to became damp and cold; when it was warm and sunny, the walls became hot and sticky. I suppressed my thoughts, not wanting Jason to sense my mood. I was getting older and more aware of our lives, and becoming jealous of everyone around us.

"Let's go outside now and play in the woods behind my house." Jason was grabbing me by the hand.

After playing a round of hide and seek in the woods, Jason stopped me. "I have an idea of a new game we can play."

"What's that?" I asked.

"It's called show and tell." Jason explained that a friend of his had taught him how to do it. In show and tell, each person took a turn asking the other to show them a body part. I was unsure, but Jason said everyone played it and I shouldn't be a wimp.

"Okay, I suppose, how bout I ask you first."

"Sounds good to me," Jason exclaimed.

"Okay, show me your elbow," I said.

"My elbow? You silly, you don't get it," Jason laughed. "You can't ask me to show you something that you can already see. The idea is to see something that's covered by my clothes."

"Okay," I said, "show me your big toe."

Now Jason was getting frustrated. "Dummy, I'm going to go first. Show me your right boob." Jason said.

I didn't feel comfortable, but I didn't want to disappoint Jason. I felt like he was a real friend, and unlike so many other kids, he didn't care about how poor we were, or that I didn't have a mom. He didn't think it was weird that my dad didn't work, and he didn't care that I called my dad Carl. I didn't want to upset Jason and have him lose interest in me as a friend. I slowly pulled down the right side of my shirt and gave him a quick glance.

"Wait, that was too quick," Jason quickly said, "you've got to give me a good look."

By the time we were done with the game, we'd both been more or less naked. We even tried kissing, but fortunately, neither of us knew how to do it, and thought it was kind of gross. We promised not to tell anyone that we played show and tell, but said we'd try it again.

We spent the rest of the afternoon by the creek, tossing stones in the water to see how many skips we could get. I was a pretty good skipper from all the practice with my dad, and Jason couldn't beat me.

"Okay, let's have another contest," I yelled. "Stand right here and see how far you can skip this rock."

I handed Jason a nice flat rock. Jason accused me of making everything into a competition.

"You've got the better rock, switch with me."

"I'm not switching with you, if you don't like your rock, find a better one." I said to him.

"Okay, fine, I'm not going to be ready until I've found the flattest best rock."

Jason spent the next ten minutes digging through all the rocks, trying to find the perfect one. In the end, I beat him anyway.

"You owe me," I said.

"Owe you? I don't owe you anything, you cheat," He argued. We laughed all the way back home, Jason accusing me of cheating at every game we played together.

~~\\ ^~

I wonder if Jason qualified as my first boyfriend. We were only seven years old, and even though showing each other body parts wasn't exactly appropriate, we didn't know the difference, and seeing him naked had no sexual meaning to me. We were both more thrilled to do something different, and had quickly returned to our comfortable game of rock skipping. Jason was just as competitive as I was, and we bonded over the thrill we mutually received from competing just for the sake of it. Jason couldn't beat me at running, but he loved to try.

Jason gave me that security I needed as a male friend. My dad would always be my best friend, but he was my dad, and he represented the longing I had for more. Jason provided companionship, with a secure and traditional family. I loved hanging out at his house when his mom and dad came home, just to witness the routines of a normal household.

My attraction to Mike was formed over our similar love of competition; the fact that we could compete against each other without animosity made me think we could be husband and wife. Neither of us was good enough at triathlons to qualify at the national level, but we received similar gratification from the thrill of being able to complete the long distance competitions.

The amount of training we did – an hour before work, an hour after work, and eight hours both Saturday and Sunday – required an obsessive level of discipline and determination. I hadn't realized how much value I ascribed in a relationship to family and sexual attraction. I didn't respect Mike's family from the beginning, and it wasn't long before my respect towards him also began to wane. With the loss of respect, I also lost any sexual attraction that ever existed. I was confused at how important a love of competition was in any relationship I would have. It had been my personal defining characteristic my whole life, but did it need to be the defining characteristic of my spouse? I realized the importance of family and family values; having grown up always wanting more of a family, I needed to find someone who had a strong family, and wanted to build a strong family.

It's difficult to say when my relationship with Brooks began. We met through a mutual friend at Freedom shortly after I moved to Boston, and instantly became friends. A large group of us shared a ski house in Vermont. Brooks was the only single person. Brooks was the type of guy I probably never would have been attracted to in high school or college. He wasn't a varsity letter winner, and didn't possess a similar level of competitive drive for athletics. He was your classic well-rounded athlete – above average at most every sport, without excelling at any one thing. He occasionally went to the gym, but would stop after half an hour for fear of stressing his body too much, and would only work out every other day. He claimed he needed the rest. He seemed to do everything well, but didn't take anything to an extreme. His moods were similarly well balanced, and he always appeared to be calm and happy. He paid no attention to how he dressed, and was regularly seen in a pair of jeans, Tevas during the summer, and a tattered old fleece. There was something attractive about his carefree appearance and grubby look that was attractive. He was the type of guy almost everyone liked – very easy going, could talk about anything, had a good sense of humor, and was always happy. He did everything in moderation, a stark contrast to my obsessive and addictive personality. He ate three well-balanced meals a day, never snacking and rarely eating junk food; in contrast, I refused to slow down to eat during the day, and would stuff myself with anything and everything to wind down at night. I had been forced to do so while working non-stop hours to pay for college. On paper he was a stud – graduate of Yale, Wharton Business school, investment banker, and now an analyst at MMM, Freedom's closest money management competitor in town. Like all of us, he was on his way to making a lot of money. I had already met his parents and two sisters, and it was very clear he had an incredibly close-knit family. Friends would tease him for being the silver spoon baby – the kid who grew up with everything handed to him. It seemed to be a slight exaggeration, but it was clear our backgrounds were very different.

There were two distinct instances when I felt something I could only describe as weird at the time. There were ten of us up skiing one weekend in Vermont. We awoke Sunday morning to a blizzard and sub-zero temperatures. Skiing appeared to be out of the question. With nothing to do in our small condo, we all settled down in the family room, lit a big fire, and found spots on the couch to relax and read. I ended up next to Brooks, and found myself unable to concentrate on my book as I listened to his breathing, sensed his smell, and felt completely distracted by his close presence.

Several weeks later, our group was turned away from the ski slopes with another sub-zero day. We piled into several cars and headed to the movie theaters. A debate ensued about what movie to see, *The Whole Nine Yards*, or *The Cider House Rules*. I was indifferent, typically being out of touch with the latest movie offerings. Mike, and most of the group, wanted to see

*The Cider House Rules*. Brooks was the lone supporter of *The Whole Nine Yards*. Almost involuntarily I changed my vote to *The Whole Nine Yards*. Mike always went along with whatever I suggested, and quickly changed his vote. It had become one of his many traits that led to my lack of respect for him. The three of us went to The Whole Nine Yards. I sat next to Brooks, and once again, found myself completely distracted by his close presence. I noticed we both laughed at the same stupid jokes, with Mike chiming in seconds later so as not to be left out.

—⁓⋀⋀⁓—

I read and re read Brooks' email, excited at the offer, and now well aware of my feelings for him. Mike and I were far into the divorce process, but only several of our closest friends knew of the situation.

"Several of us might go hiking on Good Friday; wanted to see if you'd like to join." It was a completely innocent email, and more than appropriate given our friendship. I knew Mike had to work Good Friday. The email noted "several of us." I wondered whom he was referring to, but it didn't really matter. I was extremely sore from running the Boston Marathon two days prior, and the thought of hiking a mountain in three days wouldn't normally seem appealing, but I figured I could handle it. I looked around hesitantly when Brooks picked me up with only one friend along.

"Oh, Kate couldn't make it. It's just the three of us." He commented casually.

"Good." I responded too quickly. "Umm, I didn't mean good, just, oh yeah, that's fine."

"Hey, slow down you guys, what the heck!" Matt screamed ahead at us as we tripped and stumbled up the mountain.

We had been caught in a snowstorm that had quickly changed to sleet and rain as we hit the upper portions of the mountain. The conditions were downright terrible, but we were having a blast.

"Hey Matt, sorry for walking too fast." I walked back to give him some company.

"I'm holding you guys back, I'm sorry to be so pokey." The poor guy was embarrassed.

"Here, let me hold your pack for you," I offered. This only added to his shame, but he was clearly suffering from the weight of his backpack.

"Wimp, makin' the girl help you out!" Brooks was quick to chime in, mocking Matt for being out of shape. I took the pack regardless, and Brooks took off in a run, racing to reach the top of the mountain. Poor Matt was left far behind as I instantly followed after him, laughing the whole time. We continued laughing most of the way up the mountain. We all looked ridiculous, covered in mud and soaking wet from the weather. Matt didn't quite make it to the top, but joined us for the descent down. Brooks had since taken on the duty of carrying Matt's pack, and I now felt comfortable enough to chide Matt for being a wimp.

"We did it!" The three of us screamed in unison as we exited the base of the mountain and headed to the warmth of the car.

Brooks was tougher than I had realized, and I was impressed with his hiking abilities. He told me about his near death incident while hiking in Nepal, and about all the Backroads trips he had taken – hiking and camping in various regions of the world. Even though he wasn't an extreme athlete, he was definitely strong and had a similar love of the outdoors. I thought about Mike and the attraction that was formed over our love of triathlons. His abilities as a swimmer, biker, and long distance runner fooled me into thinking he was tough all around. Mike and I had traveled to Peru to hike Machu Picchu; he had spent most of the hike throwing up, unable to handle the high altitudes. I had no sympathy for him, and spent much of the trip complaining about how he was holding me back. The trip had entailed four days of hiking to reach the ruins; we hiked daily from seven in the morning until three in the afternoon. I was bored, hanging out at the campsite in the late afternoons, and would take off by myself, doing several hours of additional hiking. I chided Mike for not being able to keep up and join me; he spent his afternoons passed out in the tent. A friend had coined the term, "stamina snob" to describe me once; I looked down at everyone who didn't have my ability to go all day long.

My hands and feet were now aching from being damp and cold, and I feared frostbite. On the mountain, I was able to ignore every sensation of pain. Now on the ground, I realized how numb I really was. Brooks sensed my distress as we sat down in the car and held my hands in between his, rubbing them to get the circulation going. It was nothing like what I had felt when my teammate's dad had rubbed my feet after our fateful high-school cross-country meet in the bitter cold. I'll never forget the sensation I felt at that moment. It was too powerful to describe, but there was no mistaking it. This was more than a crush. I didn't know what to do. Here I was, married, granted in the midst of a divorce, but not exactly ready to jump into another relationship. I feigned exhaustion on the ride back to Boston, and lay down in the back seat to be alone with my thoughts. For all I knew, the feelings were one sided, and I promised myself I'd find the will power to brush aside the overwhelming emotions I felt.

That evening a group of us went out to dinner – Mike and I, Brooks, and several of our other mutual friends. I lit up instantly upon seeing Brooks again, even though it had only been several hours since we'd last been together.

———◌◌◌———

As the divorce progressed, Brooks and I eventually admitted

the feelings we felt toward each other. Fortunately it wasn't one-sided. We agreed that the feelings were not appropriate given my current situation, and promised to avoid each other as best we could. It was incredibly difficult. I was now living alone, now on my third short-term rental. But I was somewhat lonely, adjusting to living alone again. I plowed my energies into work, and was fortunately excelling at work, but I longed to see Brooks. We began talking on the phone each evening. Our thirty-minute nightly conversations soon turned to hour and two hour long discussions. I was now sleeping better than ever, a true sign my insomnia had been related to distress about Mike. But regardless, I was sleep deprived from phone conversations that began to continue into the morning hours. The depth of individual I found in Brooks was exactly the missing character trait that I had failed to identify in Mike. I still struggled to understand the mistake I had made, and I was unable to coherently explain it to others. Even Brooks began to question me on why I was leaving Mike, and how I had not seen the issues prior to getting married.

My insomnia returned for several days as I wrestled with my upcoming trip and whether or not I should go. It was a three-day healthcare conference in Phoenix, and Brooks was also signed up to attend. We worked for competing mutual funds, and although I traveled regularly for work, I rarely saw him at the various conferences I attended. We had discussed the Arizona conference in advance. Would it be too difficult to see each other after avoiding each other for so many months? In the end we agreed we could handle it like adults; we were there for meetings, and the odds of us even being in the same conference room together were small.

I returned to my hotel room the first evening after a long company dinner. I was exhausted from the time zone, the flight, and a long day of meetings.   As soon as I undressed, the phone rang.

"Hey, it's me, you're back.  Let's go grab a drink."

My heart accelerated as I listened to Brooks on the other end.  "It's 10 pm, aren't you going to bed soon?"

I had to decline, at least this first night.

"C'mon, I'm wired."

I declined again; I was trying to be strong.

"Ok then, let's go hiking in the morning before the meetings start.

"Now you've got a good idea."   I responded excitedly. Hiking seemed more innocent.

"Only if you go running with me first though."  I added. We agreed to meet at 6 am.

He tried one last time, "and I'll see you at the bar in 5 minutes for one quick drink."

I was secretly hoping he'd try a last time, and relented. We stayed out until 2 am, talking incessantly.  Other colleagues were also at the bar, and we were only business associates having a good time.   There was nothing unusual about our being out together.

We both got upgraded on the flight home, and shared adjoining seats for the five-hour trip back.  My feelings towards Brooks had become incredibly strong, and suppressing them became futile.  But I kept telling myself the timing was wrong. My divorce was not yet complete, and we were only six months into what my lawyer had assured me would be more than a year long process.  I lay my head on the armrest next to Brooks and began to cry.  I tried to hide my tears, but I also wanted him to know how I felt, and the emotional anguish I felt over what I would soon tell him.

"Are you crying?" he placed his hand on my shoulder.

"I'm just tired, I'm going to take a nap," I lied.

I let the tears stream down my face, and continued to shield myself from his view.  We exited the plane, both somber from the realization that our time in Arizona was now over. I was not prepared as I walked off the plane to see Mike waiting, holding a "Welcome Home" sign. I cringed upon seeing him. He was relentless in his efforts, and his desperation only turned him off to me more.

Mike drove us both home, dropping me off last at my current rental apartment. I had eventually told him the location of my last residence on advice from Ailsa to appear more conciliatory.

"You know, it's not too late if you want to change your mind, I miss you."

"Mike, stop, please, it is too late." Fortunately he didn't try to keep me. The threats of a restraining order had sufficiently scared him. I entered my apartment, and instantly collapsed on the couch, now letting the tears flow freely. I missed Brooks, knowing I had to end the relationship to preserve everything I had built for myself. I sat down, and spent the next several hours writing him a letter.

I had grown almost overly conscientious about what other people thought, and wasn't ready to delve into a relationship with Brooks if others were likely to judge or suspect that I had cheated on Mike. I thought back to the days of school in California and being picked on for being poor. Even after we had moved out of poverty, I went out of my way to try to fool people into thinking we had more than we did. I was embarrassed that we lived in the back apartment of the house in New York and not in the whole house. I worked so many hours primarily to save for college, but also to be able to buy nice clothes and fit in with the popular crowd. I had finally succeeded, was working in a top profession, and had many friends. I wasn't willing to risk having people look down on me or suspect that I wasn't everything my image conveyed – smart, successful, moral, and honest. A part of me wanted to run away with Brooks and forget about everything I had worked so hard to obtain; but I was too practical and focused to do that. I had to stop things before they went too far, and was too much of a wimp to do it in person. I had acquired my dad's love for writing, and always resorted to letters when I wanted to share my feelings. I wanted Brooks to know how much I cared, and I wanted him to know why I couldn't act on it. The only way I could explain myself intelligibly was in writing.

My letter to Brooks made me even more determined to get Mike out of my life forever. I had to get my stuff out of the apartment he was still living in, and it was time to give into all his monetary demands.

~∧∧~

"Get off the steps, or I will call the police." Mike pushed me backwards, almost causing me to fall down the flight of stairs leading up to our brownstone.

I hadn't lived in the apartment we owned jointly for close to a year now, but we still owned it, and other than my clothes, most of my possessions were still inside. I had the key, but was always too scared to venture over there when he might be home. Several times I had driven by at random hours when I assumed he should have been traveling for work, but the lights were always on, and I didn't dare go inside.

A colleague from work had volunteered to help me pick up my things, and when we pulled up in his truck, I was surprised to see Mike hanging out on the steps.

"What are you doing here?" He glared at me. "Oh, and I see you've brought a pretty new boyfriend with you.

My friend Tom, who was helping me out was quite good looking, but I hadn't even considered that Mike might be suspicious of our relationship. I was actually glad to have him think that we might be a couple; it meant he hadn't figured anything out about Brooks.

"Oh, and good for you, looks like you found yourself a rich boyfriend." He eyed Tom's Lexus truck.

"Mike, I'm just here to pick up my stuff. It's over, now it's time for you to give me my things." I couldn't even look at him.

He pushed against my shoulders again. This time Tom had come right up behind me to brace any potential fall.

"Just give her the stuff and we'll be out of your way." Tom tried to help, but Mike only gave him a shove as well.

"Get both of your asses out of here, or I will call the police. I'm not kidding you. I'll convince them you're trying to rob me."

I looked into his eyes, feeling momentary guilt about everything that had happened. He looked so pitiful. But my feelings of anger and resentment were too strong to feel more than a second of sorrow for him.

"Forget it Tom, let's get out of here." I wasn't giving him the satisfaction of thinking I even cared much about my stuff.

In the end, I gave him everything - every penny of our money, the house, the car, and all of my personal possessions. I thought back to our move out of the lean-to with my dad, and the only possessions we had that had all fit into a duffel bag. I had only a duffel bag's worth of stuff after my marriage with Mike was officially over. I would never get to reminisce with my children over my childhood photo albums.

# Chapter 4 - Determination

To pay for college and business school I had started working as soon as anyone would hire me. The first thing I was able to do was deliver papers. I applied for a paper route with the newspaper my dad wrote for, *The Daily Gazette*. It was one of the meatier papers in the area, but it also cost more than the local paper, which I figured would mean larger tips. I started with thirty houses and worked my way up to fifty. I dove into the opportunity, deciding that I would be the best paper deliverer they ever had. Before the day of my first delivery, I typed up a letter to each of my customers. "My name is Yola, and I am your new paper girl. I will be delivering your paper between five and six am. Please let me know where you would like it, and I will do my best to accommodate everyone. I will be collecting on Sunday mornings between nine and ten am. If you will not be home then, please leave the money in an envelope by your front door. Thank you and I look forward to serving you." I was proud of my letter and showed it to my dad for approval.

"Way to go kiddo, that's the way to approach a new business. Always start with a good impression."

I was eager to please my dad and excited to make my own money.

⁓ᴧᴧ⁓

Ring. Ring. It was Sunday, my collection day. Delivering the papers took a total of forty minutes. I was hoping that because of my letter I could collect in no more than an hour. Wishful thinking. I kept pressing the buzzer. It looked like they were home, and I could see the blinking of the television inside. A man peered around the door, opening it just a crack.

"What do you want?" I could only see his eyes and the top of his head, a huge mat of gray hair.

"I'm here for the Gazette collection." I tried to say in my friendliest voice.

"I don't have any money." The man grumbled.

Are you kidding me? "It's only $1.25." I stuck my foot in the doorway as he attempted to quickly close it.

"Like I said, I don't have any money, come back another day."

I had no choice but to walk away, and this time he almost clipped my foot pushing the door shut. I tried to keep my head up as I walked down the street to the next house. I'd been working on collecting for over two hours, and only had eleven dollars and seventy-five cents. My bill was due at the Gazette for my weekly papers the next day, and I was already behind from last week. The next house should be more reliable I thought. There was a swing set out back, and I figured anyone with kids wouldn't claim to not have any money. I rang the bell, waiting in anticipation as I heard the sound of footsteps.

I stood in shock not knowing what to do. A young man had opened the door. He had rollers in his hair, make up on his face, and was wearing a pink bathrobe. The pink bathrobe was open, exposing absolutely everything. My legs turned to jelly, as I struggled to run away.

"How'd ya do?" My dad greeted me at the door. "You sure were gone a long time, I hope you got a lot of money."

My dad had no idea I was building up a debt with the Gazette.

"Good." I pushed by him and walked back towards my room. "I have a lot of homework to do." I knew the homework excuse would face no argument.

I applied the next day for paper routes with the other two local newspapers. I didn't know how else to pay off my debt with the Gazette, and I figured the customers would eventually pay. Within a week I had the responsibility of delivery one hundred and fifty newspapers. The first delivery came to our house at four thirty in the morning. I had to leave for school at eight am. The only way to make sure I could get all my papers delivered and still get to school on time was to start at four thirty in the morning. The first couple of times it would take a whole three hours to deliver all the papers. I stole a shopping cart from the local Price Chopper and filled the cart with all my papers. No matter the season I would wear a winter hat and wrap a scarf most of the way around my face. I was fearful of seeing someone I knew while out delivering papers in a shopping cart. I was embarrassed to have such a large paper route. Most of my friends who also had paper routes only had them as a lesson in responsibility. They weren't actually trying to make money. One day I got the idea to ditch the shopping cart and take one bag full of papers at a time. I would run between houses, and then once the bag was emptied, I would run back home to fill up a second bag. The whole route took about fifteen different loads. But it cut over an hour off my delivery time. I soon had a system that worked. Instead of dropping off a letter to tell my customers when I would be collecting, I collected every evening. I devoted thirty minutes each night to walking my route. That way I was sure to eventually catch every customer home. Soon I was making pretty good money with my paper routes. I went on to have three paper routes at a time for four years. All the other paper deliverers were much younger than me, and I moved up the hour I delivered to decrease the odds of seeing anyone I knew.

—∧∧—

As soon as I was old enough, I took a job waitressing at Friendly's, while still continuing the paper routes. Because Friendly's didn't serve alcohol, they hired starting at age fourteen. They gave me the 6-10 p.m. shift three nights a week, and the six to midnight shift Friday and Saturday nights. My dad wasn't happy that I would no longer be home for dinner, and most of the time he wouldn't even see me all day; I went to Friendly's straight from track practice. But he knew he couldn't argue with me when it came to my obsession with making money. "But Carl, you told me I had to make money to save for college," I would say every time he questioned my work hours.

The Grateful Dead concert was Saturday night, and I knew Friendly's would be packed on Saturday night. I showed up for my shift extra early to make sure I could get the best section. The best section was in the front of the restaurant; the tables seemed to turn quicker up front, and the more tables you could serve in a night, the more in tips you could earn.

"Hey Yola, so glad you are here. Mary and Brian called in sick, and we literally have no wait staff tonight. I've made a bunch of calls, but I can't get a hold of anyone."

"Are you kidding, the Grateful Dead are playing tonight. It will be packed here later." I looked at my manager shocked. How could I handle the whole restaurant by myself, there were more than forty tables.

"I don't know what to tell you, but we'll figure it out somehow."

"Miss, can we get our order in?" A loud group was signaling me from across the restaurant.

"Hey Miss, we ordered our sundaes ten minutes ago."

Another table was pulling on my polyester navy uniform, trying to get my attention from behind.

The Friendly's uniform was a blue and white checkered polyester dress that was extremely form fitted on top, and flared around the knees. It was likely one of the most unattractive dresses anyone could imagine. But one benefit of the material was that it came out of the washer practically dry. We were required to buy our own uniforms, and I refused to buy more than one; but every night my uniform was covered in ice cream and chocolate sauce. All I had to do was rinse it off and hang it to dry for five minutes.

"Miss, can we get some water over here?"

I was literally running through the restaurant in my waitress sneaker shoes. Another addition to the beautiful uniform that was required was matching blue or white uniform shoes. They were only sold at the uniform supply store, and although they were ugly as heck, they were quite comfortable, and you were able to dash along slippery floors without falling.

The restaurant was one hundred percent full, all forty tables, and had already turned over numerous times. It was after midnight, the normal closing time, but the manager had decided to stay open since people continued flowing in.

Reeses Pieces sundaes, Fribbles, Double Cheeseburgers, Fish a Majigs. They were ordering it all tonight, and in large quantities. It felt like all fifty thousand people that had attended the Grateful Dead concert decided to go to Friendly's. My apron pockets had already filled with bills from tips twice; I had to empty it each time into my duffel bag.

"I'm coming, I'm moving as fast as I can." I screamed to anyone that was listening. I ran through the restaurant, balancing three sundaes on my tray, just to show all the customers how diligently I was working for them.

"Hey, cute butt!" A large table of guys had started to drive me crazy with the ogling and wise comments. But I knew I couldn't say anything. I had to play the game; it wasn't worth risking the tip.

In the summer, I supplemented my Friendly's job with whatever work I could get.    I waitressed at a dumpy pizza joint in town. They paid me all in cash - $1.40 an hour plus tips. As with any waitressing job, it was all about the tips, and I didn't care what the hourly wage was. I got another job at a shoe shop in the kid's section; I hated the process of trying to get a kid to keep their foot still long enough to measure it, but the pay was pretty good. None of the jobs paid very well, so whenever I could, I took on any supplemental work I could find; I was constantly scouring the help-wanted section. I worked several weeks telemarketing; it was probably one of the worst gigs I've ever had. Spending hours calling people, only to get constantly hung up on, wasn't much fun. I did inventory work at Montgomery Wards for a while. Every several months, all the big department stores would hire people on a contract basis to help organize the stockrooms and log everything they had into notebooks. It was terribly boring, but they would let you do it during odd hours, so I could work it into my busy schedule. The one gold mine I found was working banquets at the hotel in town. A good friend's father was a manager at the Ramada Resaissance hotel, and got me a gig working special functions. No one cared that I was under age, and all I had to do was help set up and breakdown for the events. The last oddball job I did was paint signs for stores. Many of the stores on Broadway in town had fold up signs that they would place on the sidewalk in front of the store. A friend's mom, who owned a store in town, knew I was artistic, and had asked me if I'd be interested in painting the sign for her store. I used the experience to market my trade to all the other stores in town, and ended up painting signs for half a dozen of the downtown businesses.

I finally got sick from working too many hours and not sleeping; after the third day of continuing work despite a fever of one hundred and two, I called in sick to the pizza shop. The manager told me he'd fire me if I didn't show up; I got fired from a job at the age of fifteen.

I was finally old enough to apply for real jobs – I ditched Friendy's, the paper routes, and all the other oddball jobs and cobbled together a schedule that allowed barely even enough time to sleep – my schedule was six days a week, starting at 9 a.m., and finishing after 4 a.m. But I started making a lot of money, and saved almost all of what I earned.

—⁓ᴧᴧ⁓

Just one more bite. Okay, just one more bite. I'd almost finished the whole half-gallon of ice cream – Edy's vanilla raspberry swirl. I drove Pearl crazy, taking up half the freezer, as I insisted on having at least three or four containers handy on any given day. Pearl loved to cook and freeze, always prepared for who knows what; the space I took up in the freezer allowed her little room to store the many meals she was saving.

It was 4:15 in the morning, and I'd just returned home from cocktail waitressing after my hostessing shift from five to ten p.m. New York had recently extended the hour at which bars were allowed to serve alcohol from two a.m. to four a.m., giving me the opportunity to make hundreds more in tips each night. The customers were exceptionally wasted after two a.m., and average tip size tended to increase through the night. With no break between jobs since my nine a.m. start, I never took the time to eat anything. Eating slowed me down, and made me sluggish. I had a lot more energy by not eating all day. I always looked forward to my half-gallon of ice cream each night, knowing I could justify consuming the whole container. It was light, and the entire half-gallon totaled less than two thousand calories. It was my only two thousand calories in a twenty-four hour period; I figured it wasn't as bad as it sounded. Besides, I was getting a healthy share of calcium, valuable for my running career.

I polished off the half-gallon, feeling satiated and exhausted. A friend had told me that milk, when warmed, created an enzyme similar to the one found in sleeping medicines. The ice cream seemed to always be what I needed to wind down after my chaotic day. Before going to sleep I always had to count my tips from the night. Tips from hostessing were usually twenty, fifty, and one hundred dollar bills – I separated those out first – six twenties, two fifties, and one one hundred dollar bill - $320 from hostessing; it had been a good night. The key was always getting one one hundred dollar tip. The super-wealthy couldn't be bothered to make a reservation, and I was always ready with my canned speech for suckering them into slipping me a bribe. "Oh, I'm so sorry sir, we are booked solid for the night. I really don't know if there's anything you could do to convince me to make room for you." I would give them a sweet smile, and then pretend to study my reservation pad intently, letting a look of concern spread across my face as I checked off each table on the chart, indicating that they were all taken. It usually worked every time; the part I had little influence over was how big the bribe would be. I wouldn't budge for anything less than $20, but I figured $20 was worth pissing off another party that had gone to the effort of making a reservation. Hostessing had always seemed to be an easy job. What did you have to do other than stand there with a fake smile pasted across your face and happily greet each party? But I soon learned there was much more to it than that. A good hostess almost needed a degree in statistical modeling. To manage the flow of patrons in and out of a restaurant effectively required accurately, to within fifteen minutes, predicting how long a party would occupy a table. To let a table sit idle for more than fifteen minutes was absolute failure in the world of hostessing experts. Beyond predicting each table's mealtime, it was imperative to seat each particular party with the waiter or waitress that would be able to get them out of the restaurant most quickly. The romantic couple that seemed to be out to dinner for a night of peace and quiet was best paired with the chatty wait staff. They'd be sure to get irritated by the, "so where are you all from? Oh, what a coincidence, my cousin also grew up there…" and abort quickly after dessert. The larger groups were best paired with the quiet and efficient wait staff. They'd be sure to move the party along between courses. There was nothing worse than the three hour meal. Parties who sat for three hours or more would screw up the entire model. The model was programmed to have each table turn three times in an evening, with the first seating at five p.m., and the last no later than 9:30 p.m. A three hour meal would bring the number of turns down to one; you couldn't even squeeze in a second turn. Parties who came in after 9:30 p.m. weren't worth the effort; it was impossible to get them out of the restaurant in less than an hour and a half, and they'd disrupt the whole transition of the restaurant from quiet dining room to rowdy club.

I worked studiously on the art of loitering and listening, trying to both predict how much longer before a table left, and to encourage them to leave. However, it was an imperfect science, and I could never get it quite right. I consistently frustrated patrons, telling them it would likely be only an additional ten minutes, and then having thirty minutes elapse. I often told parties which table they were waiting for, encouraging them to do their own loitering.

Pennell's had twenty tables, seating one hundred and twenty guests at a time. I had the math worked out to a science. If I could turn each table three times, I could generate at least five hundred dollars in tips for the wait staff, and usually half of that amount for myself in bribes; but only if everything went according to plan. If I was caught purposely giving away someone's table for a bribe, I could screw up my whole night with irate customers.

I counted my cocktail waitressing tips next. The one-dollar bills were all crumpled up in the pockets of my apron. I dumped them all onto the bed, and then began to unfold them one by one, stacking them on top of each other. It looked like a fairly bad night; I could tell without even counting, just by the size of the stack.

Each night, when we would transform Pennell's from a fancy restaurant to a bar, we would set up a stage in the middle of the restaurant and pull out the karaoke machine. I would get onstage with another waitress, rallying the crowds to start their drinking, with our rendition of "Mickey." "Oh Mickey, you're so pretty, don't you understand…" The two of us would go back and forth, passing the microphone and dancing around the stage. We performed the same act every night, often to the usual set of regulars; they never seemed to get bored of it. It was rarely long before someone from the crowd started a clapping chant, and pretty soon everyone in the restaurant would join in. I usually performed Carly Simon's, "You're So Vain," solo after Mickey, always screaming as loud as I could when our town, Saratoga, was mentioned in the song. By that time, we'd typically excited enough people to join in on the karaoke, and that was all it took to get the drinks flowing.

But this particular night, there was a big crowd of underage drinkers in the audience. I managed to piss off a large group by refusing to serve several of their underage friends, and the whole party ended up stiffing me. There were probably twenty of them in total, enough to kill the night. I counted my stack – eighty-nine dollars, not terrible, but far from my best night.

I crashed at 4:30 a.m., in time to get my four hours of sleep before I had to get up for work the next morning. The alarm woke me at 8:45 a.m. I jolted out of bed, hurrying to get to Skidmore College for my 9 a.m. job. I had suckered a good family friend, the head of the economics department at Skidmore, to give me a job doing economics research. It was painfully boring, and barely paid at all, but I knew I had to do something for my resume. The current project I was working on was looking up and recording every oil spill that had ever occurred. The professor I was working with had a theory that oil spills were correlated with temperature changes. I had to record when the oil spill occurred, what month and year it was, and what the temperature was on the particular day. I was at least learning how to run regressions, which I figured would be useful one day.

I left Skidmore at twelve noon, rushing home as quickly as possible to wheel my cart into town. I would only have several hours to sell my hand-painted t-shirts on Broadway, and didn't want to miss the busy lunch hour. I had bought a summer permit for five hundred dollars, and leased a wooden cart that I was able to wheel from home. I looked a bit ridiculous pushing a cart the size of a car down the street, but if I jogged while pushing, I could get the cart to town and set up within thirty minutes. I had to run ever so carefully, so as to not send all the shirts stacked on top of the cart from flying into the street.   I had one day a week off from Pennell's, and I used most of the day to paint my shirts. I could paint several shirts in an hour, and each shirt generated a fifteen-dollar profit.   I figured it would give me some entrepreneurship on my resume; something that might be valuable down the road.

─∿∿─

I nervously anticipated my upcoming industry review as my Freedom internship concluded. The industry review was meant to be an exhaustive and thorough analysis of the industry you were assigned.   My industry was office products, companies involved in the distribution of office products to corporations. The industry had evolved from one where small local shops personally delivered paper, pens, ink cartridges, etc. to local businesses, to one in which large companies had bought up all the small local shops and consolidated them.   There were now only a handful of companies across the country, all with fleets of trucks, delivering paper and pens to the hundreds of corporations across the country.   I had taken the bold and risky position of attempting to claim there was accounting fraud in the industry. Following the rapid consolidation, it was easy for a company to pad the books, as the numbers could get quite complicated integrating numerous companies into one business. I knew making such a statement as a lowly intern was risky, but at the same time, I knew strategically, to get the full-time job, I had to go out on a limb and prove myself to be original. I stayed up night after night, working around the clock to prove my thesis. I pored through 10Q's and 10K's (filings that companies are required to make with the Securities and Exchange commission that contain all required financial statements), my eyes blurring over from the small print.

The actual industry review had to be a document no longer than ten pages. I could have easily written a one hundred page report, but consolidating it down to ten pages was the hardest aspect of the assignment. It was the nature of Freedom; you had to be simple and to the point. Busy portfolio managers didn't need to know all the minutiae; they wanted the conclusion, and they wanted to see the ten or twenty graphs that backed up your thesis. They didn't want to see your data, or all the analysis that went on in the middle of the night; they figured that if you knew your industry well enough, the quality of the work would be apparent.

You had to present your ten page document in front of a room of over one hundred people; all the portfolio managers and analysts at the firm were invited to watch you shame yourself publicly. Inevitably, there would be several hard-core portfolio managers who felt it was their job to ridicule the summer interns.

I was waiting my turn, barely listening as Craig gave his industry review, summarizing the beverage business.

"Excuse me, where did you obtain the data behind that graph?" Beth, known to be one of the toughest portfolio managers, interrupted Craig mid sentence.

"Ummm, well my research assistant compiled the numbers." Craig responded meekly.

"Okay, I asked you, and I'll ask you again. Where did the data come from?" She was vicious. Her tone of voice was biting and derogatory.

"I'll have to ask the research assistant."

"You're telling me you didn't validate the data. You just took it straight from a twenty year old research assistant who's still in college?"

Craig was speechless. His face was now beat red, and he only managed to stumble a brief response saying that he'd follow up with her later. My analysis of the situation was that Craig was toast. I was next to present, and I was already sweating through my shirt. I could feel my own face growing red, and I had yet to even say a word.

In the end, my presentation went off flawlessly. I was asked a number of questions, but felt confident in my answers. And fortunately, mean Beth left me alone. I had done the best I could, and now the internship was officially over. The recruiter had informed all of us that we would receive a call letting us know whether we would be receiving full-time offers to join Freedom when we were done with business school in two months. I couldn't believe they were going to torture us into waiting that long.

I got the call two weeks after returning to school. Freedom offered me the job, and even asked if I'd be willing to work part-time during my second year at school. I jumped at the opportunity, barely listening as the recruiter went over all the terms of the offer. They would pay me $200,000 to start, more money than I could even imagine at that point, and they would fly me back and forth to Boston every week during my second year of school.

The first call I made was to my dad. I was proud to tell him my news.

⟨﹏⟩

Freedom's analyst program was a rotational program – you were assigned an industry to cover, and if you did a good job, rotated to another industry after eighteen to twenty-four months. My first industry was the homebuilders and building products companies – my responsibility was to assign buys and sells to each of the companies I was assigned, and communicate my opinions as well as all relevant news flow to the fund managers. The goal was to have your buys go up and your sells go down, with as much accuracy as possible in predicting what the companies would earn in each quarter – a simple computer program tracked your success rate. You were constantly measured, with a score that tracked how good you were. Everyone in the firm could see who was doing the best on any given day. The pressure was intense, but the rewards were high; the goal was to forecast the future in your industry correctly, and be moved on to another industry as soon as possible. After covering a wide range of industries, you would then be eligible to manage diversified money – the highly coveted and very lucrative job at the firm. I was determined to win the race and get my companies right.

I had always won by working harder than everyone else and being more efficient. I was obsessed with productivity and efficiency, and would continue to be so even when I no longer had intense work related pressure. Even my husband would never know many of the things I did to save time and be more efficient. I had figured out how to cut my shower to less than four minutes, and rarely spent more than ten minutes getting ready in the morning. I used one hand to wash my hair, and the other hand to wash my body, consolidating the process into one step. While I brushed my teeth with one hand, I used the other to apply a small application of make up. Fortunately, my hair rarely required brushing, and I was able to shake my head a little to make it look presentable. In public restrooms I didn't shut the door to the stall, and often had to jump up to shut the door before I was done; I'd realize minutes later that I had to go again, and would instead force myself to hold it in until I was sure it was enough to justify the break. I didn't believe in sitting down to any meal other than dinner, and for the most part, didn't believe in eating during the day; eating before seven at night made me sluggish, and I generally consumed more than ninety percent of my daily calories in the hour before I went to bed. I similarly didn't allow myself to drink too much during the day; the bathroom breaks that resulted weren't worth the time. In college I had taken six courses a semester while everyone else took four; it allowed me to get two degrees at once. With track practice and working a part-time job, I was unable to physically attend every class I was registered for, and would consequently rotate my attendance to make sure the professor at least had a face to identify me by. But it didn't matter – with the course outline I was able to follow along; I found that I could learn the material more efficiently by reading it on my own rather than spending the hour listening to the lecture.

In approaching the Freedom opportunity, I broke out every trick I had to be as efficient as possible, and still worked more or less all the time. I would arrive at work by eight a.m., take an hour break at six p.m. to work-out (no matter what, I had to get my work out in, and after ten straight hours working, needed the energy boost I got from exercising), and then would return to work for another three to four hours. I became a regular customer of take-out taxi, and had my dinner delivered to the office. I was able to eat and read research at the same time, effectively wasting no time on eating in any given day. I was running two marathons a year, and did most of my long-runs in the very early morning. After running the Boston Marathon several years in a row, a race that was held on a Monday, I figured out how to barely make the twenty-six mile race a day off from work. The race started at eleven a.m., allowing me to get up early and work from home. I took the public bus the forty-minute ride to the start line, and would bring research reports to read on the bus ride. After running for a little over three hours, I would dash back to my apartment, which was fortunately only several blocks from the finish line, take my three minute shower, and arrive at work a little after three p.m., still giving me a good seven or eight hour work day ahead. One year I ran three marathons in a year. I had been disgusted by my performance at the Washington D.C. marathon, and to make up for my poor time, registered for the Rhode Island marathon, held exactly two weeks after Washington. I knew it was a lot to do two marathons within two weeks of each other, but I was determined to better my time. I was scheduled to attend a work conference in Phoenix the day after Rhode Island, and to be able to run the race, drive back to Boston's airport, and make the flight to Phoenix, I had to run the race in less than three hours and fifteen minutes. I sailed through the finish line in three hours and six minutes, literally ran straight to the car, and sped eighty miles an hour to the airport. I made the flight within twenty minutes of take-off, and ended up being up for more than twenty-four hours that day. After arriving in Phoenix, I was wired, and had to prepare for my meetings the next day.

I did everything I could to stand out from the large analyst team that Freedom employed; there were seventy-five other domestic analysts, all of whom were well- educated and competitive individuals. To befriend the CEO's and CFO's of the companies I covered, I thoroughly researched their backgrounds well in advance of meeting them. I discovered that several of the managers of my companies were also runners. My first meeting with one CEO was a run through Washington D.C; our tight relationship was formed when we raced each other up the steps of the Capitol – I let him win. From there on, I became the first call he took, and he connected me with every source I needed to predict the future of the industry correctly. Another CEO of one of my companies was an ex Olympic hurdler; we challenged each other to runs and quickly became friends. He spent hours with me, sharing his many insights into the industry. Beyond the management teams of the companies I covered, I worked to find any and every source that would help me get more information to correctly predict the future of my companies. I talked to plumbers, contractors, electricians, and everyone involved with the homebuilding companies; I spent many days in Washington D.C., meeting with every economic forecasting firm related to residential construction. Late night at the office, I downloaded every data source I could find to model a regression that could help to predict what indicator was most relevant in predicting the housing industry. After a year at Freedom, I was voted as one of the top ten analysts in the industry by Institutional Investor magazine, and was featured with the nine other candidates in the August edition of their magazine. The race to be number one continued and never let up during my first five years at Freedom. After correctly predicting the downfall of the banking sector, I was moved to my third industry in a record nine months. I was assigned to be the sector leader of the whole health care sector – a position that indicated you were one of the five or ten most senior analysts at the firm, and a position that came with the added responsibility of overseeing the team of analysts in your sector. The firm was short-handed, and asked me if I could cover two sectors at once and manage four different funds. I was thrilled, and didn't even consider that the workload could be too much to handle; I would figure out how to be even more efficient. I was responsible for managing a total of eleven billion dollars of health-care money.    I was featured in Forbes, Kiplinger Magazine, and the New York Times. "Yolanda is no average analyst.....she gets right to the heart of the matter and has great instincts." My pay tripled in my third year on the job, and then in the fourth year doubled again. My career was at a peak, I had made several million dollars, and I loved my job.

# Part II

# Chapter 5 — First homes

"C'mon kiddo, let's pack it up." We were leaving our lean-to.

"Where are we going this time?" I cried.

"No complaining, just get your stuff together, it's time to move on."

I'd been crying all morning. It was Saturday morning - the morning that Jean usually came down from the house and gave me one of her home baked scones. Jean had become like a mother to me. When I came home from school and my dad was out, I'd visit Jean. She didn't seem to mind, and always had something fresh baked to share. One day at school I'd been pushed around again by Sandra and her clique.

"She's dirty!" They had yelled to each other. "Let's get her."

I came home with bruises all over my knees, covered in dirt. My dad didn't tolerate crying after my many bullying incidents.

"It's all part of growing up," he would say as he casually walked away; he never offered any amount of sympathy. I didn't appreciate my dad's insistence on being tough for years. But his techniques turned me into the kid who could bounce back from any setback; I looked down on people who were too weak to handle difficult situations. I would ultimately learn how difficult it was to be tough on a kid; I would never be able to be as tough as my dad was.

After a bullying incident, Jean would give me a big hug and apply a washcloth to my bruises while I sat on her lap. "Don't worry Yola, you're better than them," she would say, "They might push you around, but I bet you're smarter than all of them, and I know you'll be more successful."

I always cherished her words. I was determined to be successful, and one day I knew I would be able to show those girls off. Sometimes, all that would keep me going was my ability to visualize. I'd imagine myself in a high-powered job, often smiling while I daydreamed in school. My images would seem so real that I'd forget about the present. I later learned that one of the girls who had always picked on me got accidentally pregnant several times in high-school, and was a regular at the abortion clinic. I thought of her when I ended up at an abortion clinic for completely different reasons. I came to believe that if you never had to overcome adversity in life, you were destined to become lazy and expect things to happen for you. My biases would prove to be overly harsh and judgmental, and I had to work to set them aside and make exceptions. "But what about Jean and Larry? I'm going to miss them." I cried.

"Jean and Larry will still live here, and we can come and visit them. Now let's get a move on. We have a lot to do today."

Once again, I had no idea where we were going. I was comfortable in our lean-to, and I loved having Jean around. My dad didn't explain anything, so I only feared the worst. Perhaps he had gotten in a fight with Larry and they were kicking us off their land. Perhaps we were escaping California, like we had escaped Vietnam years ago. How far would we go this time?

Larry helped us move, driving us with our two duffel bags of clothes, several milk crates we used for furniture, two mattresses tied to the back of his truck, and a garbage bag full of bedding and towels. These were all of our possessions. He drove us into town, and then turned down some back roads I'd never seen. Dust flew up into the air as we veered onto a dirt road. I gripped the seat, scared of all the dogs that came out to greet us. One house looked like they had five or six dogs. They all charged the truck at once. We had to stop and Larry sprayed a water bottle, causing them to dash in different directions. We came to the end of the dirt road and stopped in front of a small shack. It was several colors from multiple attempts to re paint it. The original color appeared to be pink, but the pink paint had peeled off in many areas, exposing the wood boards underneath. Someone had tried to re paint it yellow, leaving it various shades of pink, natural wood, and dirty yellow. The small porch on the front was at an angle, falling off on one side. It looked to be only one or two rooms inside, and was no bigger than a small garage.

"This is our new home kiddo," my dad proudly proclaimed.

It took several seconds before I could speak; I was so excited, "this is ours? Really?" "Can we go inside? Can I see? Can I see?" Larry and Jean helped us unload our belongings onto the front porch, and then said their good byes. I was sad to say good-bye to Jean, but I was now more excited about the house. I gave her a quick hug and kiss, almost pushing past her to get a peek inside.

"Please come visit anytime." Jean called as she leaned out the truck window while they pulled away.

It would take thirty years before I was sufficiently proud and curious about the life we had led in California for us to return.

We delicately walked up the porch of our new house, careful to not hold onto the railings that were about to fall off. The interior was meager at best, but it was far better than the lean-to and the packing crate we had lived in. There were four small rooms. The kitchen and living room were combined, with dingy old white appliances coated in black grease. A small hallway connected the kitchen/living room area to a bathroom without a door, and two small bedrooms. One was barely large enough for even my mattress, but it would be mine. I couldn't imagine having a bedroom all to myself. The whole place smelled of must and left over take out food. The bathroom toilet bowl was coated brown, and the sink was backed up with dingy water.

"This is it kiddo, this is our new home. I figured we were ready to live in a real house."

I smiled, almost wanting to hug him; my dad and I never displayed any physical affection towards each other. Instead I danced around the kitchen saying, "Wow, a real house, we have a real house!"

My dad had been putting aside a portion of his welfare check every month into an envelope he called his house fund. It had taken five years, and he had saved enough for the first months' rent and deposit. When I was at school, he had been busy walking the five miles into town to scout out apartments and houses for rent.

After we put our things inside, my dad went alone into town to buy some cleaning supplies. I took the opportunity to explore the neighborhood. We were at the end of the street, set back far enough that a passerby would miss our house at first glance. All the houses on the street were characteristically similar – small, one to two room shacks, many in desperate need of repair. Most had porches, all sinking under the weight of broken refrigerators, bicycles, and an eclectic mix of junk piled high. The entire street looked like a big junkyard.

"Hey, are you new here?"

I was startled as I turned around to see a boy my age walking toward me. He was covered in what looked to be bike grease, and had bruises all over his knees. He was even skinnier than me.

"Yeah, we just moved into the house at the end of the street." I smiled.

"Oh good, some cranky old man used to live there. Hey, want to see my house?"

I hesitated, but didn't want him to think I was scared. "Sure, I guess. My dad probably won't be back for a little while."

We could barely open the door into his house. The whole porch was strewn with plastic ride on toys, beat up bicycles coated in grease with their chains hanging off, and what looked to be boxes of old cat litter.

"Wow, you have a lot of stuff." I didn't know what to say once we were inside. It was the most disgusting house I could ever imagine. There were clothes tossed all over, bags of old food piled on top of the table, the sink was overflowing with dirty dishes, and the entire place smelled like cat urine.

"Do you have a cat?"

"We have four cats. Here, come meet them." Tommy led me to the back room where the cats lived. The floor was covered with cat litter and what looked to be week old cat poop. I started to breathe through my mouth so I didn't have to smell the awful stench. "This is Minky, Micky, and Monica."

"Wow, all M names, that's cool." I didn't know what else to say.

Tommy continued to lead me from room to room, each of which was equally disgusting. I was relieved when he finally said that I should probably go back home because he had homework to do. I wondered how he could possibly do any homework amidst all the junk.

Homework was the most important thing to my dad. Even if there was no homework, he required me to review what I had done, and prepare for what might be upcoming. Homework time was always a designated time, to be done away from any distractions. My dad would both review and augment my homework, a practice he continued until he went back to work and didn't have enough time in the day. As much as I hated homework time, and dreaded my dad's over involvement in it, I would miss that time together when it was no longer there.

My dad was angrier than I'd ever seen him when I got home.

"Where the hell were you?" He yelled.

"Who the hell do you think you are, just taking off without telling me?  Never ever do that again!"

Because he was so mad, I actually felt bad.  I didn't know what to say.

"I was just across the street.  I met the boy who lives in the white house over there." I pointed.

"I don't care where you were.  For all I knew someone had taken off with you.  I was just about to ask a neighbor to call the police."

When my dad got angry, his cheeks got all red, and his eyes had this beady look to them.  I decided it was best for me to not say anything more.

We spent the rest of the day scrubbing our new house.  It was dirtier than it looked at first.  Every corner was filled with mold and cobwebs.  The sinks had layer after layer of grime.  My dad still wasn't talking to me, so we worked in silence.  Later that day, we walked down to the corner store, and the storeowner gave me a huge bag of can tops.  I sat on the porch and made a curtain for my room door.  None of the rooms in the house had doors, and I figured this would give me a little privacy.  I had seen a curtain made of can tops at one of the stores in town, and it seemed like a great idea.  The can tops were the tabs that were on soda cans.  If you took two of them, you could clasp them together, and keep repeating until you made one long string of tabs, all connected.  I made twenty different strings of the tabs, and then nailed each string to the top of the door.  With the strings all in place, you could no longer see directly into my room.  It certainly didn't block out any sound, and all you had to do was push the strings aside to see in, but I liked it nonetheless.

That night my dad made dinner.  It was a special day, and he had picked up eggs and bacon in town.  He made the best omelets ever. His technique of adding a splash of water created an extra fluffy omelet. We ate on the front porch since we didn't yet have a kitchen table.

Finally my dad spoke, "So kiddo, what do you think?"

"I like it," I said, "This is a nice house."

We didn't say anything more that night. We sat outside until it was good and dark, looking up at the stars, and enjoying our new home.

⌒∿⌒

Brooks and I were married less than two years after my divorce was complete. Our real relationship, when we were finally able to be together openly, progressed quickly. I had never been happier; I was at the top of my career and I had finally met my soul mate.

My dad gave a speech at our wedding that had everyone laughing. I was worried he was going to give us away, and everyone would know our relationship had actually begun before the divorce was final.

"Yola and Brooks have had a way of doing everything backwards in their relationship. One day Yola called me and told me she's met this great guy. Well, I had my doubts, so when they came over, I put him through the ringer. Surprisingly, he passed. Well, next thing you know, she tells me they're building a house together. I didn't believe it, but when I visited Boston, well, boy was it true. Now, you should see this house. It's big enough to fit a bowling alley inside! After I hear about the house, she tells me they're getting married in October. I guess next they'll announce they're getting engaged."

The letter I had sent Brooks just prior to the end of the divorce had fortunately brought us closer together rather than ending our relationship. He had called me shortly after receiving it, and put his feelings on the line.

"My Mom told me if there's something or someone you

really want in life, to take the chance and let them know how you really feel." He paused, and I dared not interrupt. "I don't want to lose you, and I don't care how long it takes. I never believed I'd find what we have together, and I don't want to lose it - ever." Brooks was always to the point, never one to waste words.

I felt weak, listening to him go on. "I think you know I feel the same way, but this is so hard; I don't know what to do." My voice cracked. I'd been miserable since sending him the letter, but felt I had no choice.

We agreed to continue avoiding social gatherings together, but we knew we couldn't stop our nightly phone conversations. We spent six months without ever seeing each other in person. I lulled myself to sleep each night, imagining the day when I could lie in his arms.

Once the divorce was complete, Brooks and I began to arrange meetings. We started cautiously, still reluctant to let anyone know. We met in several locations outside of town, spending weekends together in Washington DC, Florida, and Vermont. Our relationship continued to build, and I knew I was in love. Our relationship was so different from the one I was used to. There was a mutual respect. We longed to spend every minute of every day together. I had confidence that this time it would be forever.

Brooks' parents had a second home in Florida, and I agreed to a weekend away where I would meet them. The house was only just completed, and his parents would be staying at a nearby hotel, but they offered us the house. The house would have a bed, but no other furniture. Brooks and I didn't care; we were excited for our adventure of staying in a house together.

Dinner with Brooks' parents was fun, relaxing, and comfortable. His father had recently retired as head of a financial services firm, and his mother had recently retired as a pre-school teacher. They were wealthy, active, healthy, had raised three adult children, and now were retired and enjoyed being together. Fred asked me numerous intelligent questions about my job at Freedom. Carole asked me all about my family, my friends, and what my hobbies were. They were easy to talk to, intelligent, and fun to be around.

Brooks and I were at a wedding in California. It had been three months since the finalization of my divorce, and we had only recently begun to tell friends.

"So when do you want to get married?" Brooks blurted out.

I choked on my soda. I was in shock. Although all I wanted to do was spend the rest of my life with him, I wasn't yet ready to discuss marriage.

"Um, I don't know, I hadn't really thought about it." I stammered, turning away as I felt my cheeks flush.

"Well, I was thinking next October. Tracy's wedding is in August, and we have to give her at least a month to relish the attention." Tracy was the younger of Brooks' two sisters.

We were engaged in March, a full year and two months after the finalization of my divorce. Friends welcomed our relationship as soon as we announced we were together. Friends subsequently told me what a mistake they thought I had made with Mike. The wedding was scheduled for October 26th, exactly two months after Tracy's wedding. It was wonderful, and in every way felt like the first and only wedding I would ever have.

We had started looking at houses before telling friends and family we were dating. It was a fun activity to do on weekends. But before we knew it, we had employed the services of a realtor who was actively scouting out locations. In a matter of weeks, we had closed on land and signed an agreement with a builder. It was an eighteen-month process, giving us plenty of time to tell everyone after the wedding; by that time, the house would still be in the early stages of construction. My dad almost blew it, but fortunately, the guests had all consumed plenty of drinks and didn't seem to notice the inconsistencies. We had even already had theoretical discussions about kid's names. We were careful to say, "If you had kids, what would you name them?" Rather than, "if we had kids…." But we had already agreed our mutual favorite boy/girl names were Kyle and Ashley.

We had a blast building the house together. Our shared skills as quick decision makers were useful in the house building process. There were hundreds of choices to be made; we'd sit together with the builder, ticking off one after the other. We told him we only wanted three choices for every decision that needed to be made – faucets, door handles, and moldings. Together we'd say A for that, B for this. We almost always agreed; the process was smooth and fun.

Our house turned out beautifully. We had chosen shingle style arts and crafts. It was simple and elegant. The plot of land was perfect – almost an acre, and flat, ideal for kids. We had similarly chosen the furnishings, using an interior decorator, with our A, B, and C method. We furnished the whole house with two different hour and a half meetings with the decorator.

I was both embarrassed and proud of our new home. A work colleague said to me one day, "Wow, I drove by the house you're building…..it sure is large." I smiled, not knowing what to say. He was a fellow fund manager and could certainly afford a house as large as he wanted; I didn't know how to interpret his comments. When Carl and Pearl first came to visit, my combined feelings of embarrassment and pride were most strong. I could tell they loved it, but I also sensed awkwardness.

As I started adding personal touches to our new home, one of the first things I put up in the entranceway was a picture of my first home as a kid – it was a picture of me and my dad standing in front of the house, when we had gone back to visit for my dad's 60th birthday. Next to the photo of our shack, I put a drawing Brooks had done as a kid of a house. Carole had told me that Brooks was obsessed, even as a child, with eventually marrying and moving into a typical American home with a white picket fence – he had drawn an image of his dreams at age four.

We quickly adapted to our new life in the suburbs, not missing the city a bit. I looked forward each night to returning to our house and making a fancy dinner in the kitchen; I loved the stability and comfort of sitting down to a meal together. I knew our marriage would be forever.

# Chapter 6 - Fertility

"Just gain some weight, and come back in several months."

I was in yet another gynecologist's office, listening to the same useless advice. They all assumed my petite build was the cause of our inability to get pregnant. We'd been trying for just over a year; I had read every book on how best to conceive, heeding every bit of advice I could. I had cut down on caffeine, slowed down the pace and distance of my daily runs, and even tried to lessen my stress at work. But month after month, my period would return, driving me to obsess more, and work harder to get pregnant. If only working harder could make a difference.

I had become intensely focused on wanting to create the perfect family for Brooks and myself. It consumed all my thought and energy, making it near impossible to concentrate at work. I would sit at my office desk, scouring the Internet for every article on how to get pregnant. I had researched all the ovulation predictor kits, the basal temperature theories, and had already developed a thorough understanding of the field of infertility. As soon as someone would appear in my office, I'd quickly close the screen I had on my desktop, only to reopen it to do more research as soon as they left. I was determined that we had to be the family that Brooks must have visualized in the house he drew with the white picket fence. I subconsciously began channeling my competitive energy away from work and towards having a family with Brooks. I was willing to do whatever it would take.

I went to an IVF clinic and begged them to see me. Brooks thought I was over doing it. "Just be patient, we'll get pregnant eventually," he would say.

"How do you know? We're not young anymore," I argued. It wasn't necessarily my age that I was worried about, but it was the only thing I could say that sounded rationale. It wouldn't have sounded rationale to describe the longing and void I felt after only a year of marriage. It wouldn't have sounded rational to describe the competitive drive I had towards wanting to be successful at child bearing. I couldn't look at women walking down the street pushing their baby strollers. I came to resent every friend that was getting pregnant. I blew off their baby showers, making up endless excuses. I stopped reading magazines that had pictures of young children in them. It was all I could think about.

The IVF clinic did more tests, but this time on both Brooks and me. They found an issue with Brooks' sperm. I couldn't believe it. All the months with tests only on me; I had assumed that our infertility was my fault. At first I was mad. Why didn't we test for this earlier? We could have saved so much time. Then I became resentful towards my husband. What was wrong with him? Why was everything always more difficult for me? I never told Brooks my feelings. We were a team, and this was a joint effort. But with another friend getting pregnant every day, I couldn't help it.

The good news was that because of the sperm issue we were able to move forward with IVF (in-vitro fertilization) very quickly; it was the only way we could get pregnant. Every other option that other people would have to try first was hopeless without viable sperm. I tried to charge ahead at work, not letting the time demands of IVF get in the way. I had to be at the hospital every day at seven a.m. for the daily monitoring of my hormone levels; I was always the first to arrive, starting the line that formed at 6 a.m. I brought a pile of research to read while I waited for the nurse to open the door at precisely seven, justifying the time with the work I was able to get done. The whole process took twenty minutes; if I could leave the hospital by 7:30, no one at work would know I was missing. I packed my medicines and needles in my carry on bag for business trips, making sure to stand behind all of my colleagues in the airport security line, just in case the guards had to search my bag.

"Hello everyone, I'm sorry to inform you that we will probably be on the runway another forty-five minutes before we are able to take off."

I cringed, listening to the third delay the captain had announced on our flight to Philadelphia. I sighed, looking down again at my watch. I could have predicted the time, since I'd only just looked at my watch less than a minute ago; I had been staring at the second hand, sighing dramatically, watching very minute tick by. It was all I could do to pass the time while I stressed about how I was now going to have to inject myself with the IVF medicines while our plane was en route. I had planned the trip strategically, specifically choosing the earlier flight so that I could do the injection after landing. The process required me to mix three different vials of medicine very precisely; any small error could cause the whole IVF cycle to fail. I then had to attach a two-inch needle to the syringe of medicine and insert it into my butt. I was worried I wouldn't be able to do it correctly with the movement of the plane.

"Crap!" I screamed again, this time dropping the vial I had just opened. I couldn't get one of the bottles open, and every time I tried, I ended up splashing a little bit out of the other vial. I had the various small glass containers all lined up along the edge of the tiny airplane sink; every time the plane would jerk, they'd rattle and almost spill over into the murky water that had not fully drained.

"Are you okay in there?" The stewardess knocked on the door again.

I had been in the restroom for the last twenty minutes, and had still not done the injection.

"Fine, thanks. Sorry, I'll be out soon."

I ended up haphazardly mixing together whatever I could, and pushed the needle in just as the turbulence started, causing it to bend at the last minute. I quickly pulled it out, wiping the blood off with the back of my sleeve. I felt the sting instantly, cringing as my butt muscles began to tighten.

"Everyone return to their seats. We are entering a period of choppy air." The loud voice of the captain startled me; the volume on the bathroom speaker was turned up to the maximum level.

"Miss," the stewardess was banging on the door again, "you really need to return to your seat."

"I'm coming!" I screamed, startling myself, and feeling embarrassed for snapping at her. I rushed out of the small bathroom, the glass bottles of medicine jiggling in my pocketbook as I hobbled back to my seat: I could barely walk, my muscles were now frozen from the effects of the drugs.

"Have you been running too much again?" Friends would say every day. I didn't want to tell anyone we were doing IVF; they assumed I was running too much when I limped around the office. The doctors couldn't understand why the medicine was having such an adverse reaction on my muscles, but there was nothing they could do about it. "It's a required part of the process, I'm not sure what to tell you," they would say, "It's an oil based medicine that gets poorly absorbed by the muscles." It wasn't much consolation. I would suffer the effects of the injections for years to come, with chronic muscle issues that permanently ruined my running abilities. The emotional effects would ultimately be much greater than the physical ones.

I ended up changing my work position, switching into a management job that didn't require travel. Although I chose to make the change, the partial involuntary nature of it made me feel defeated and angry. I was bitter that we couldn't easily have a child, and I couldn't continue on my uphill career climb. I was jealous of my husband for being able to march ahead without interruptions. Emotionally, he was going through his own struggles, but he wasn't forced to modify any aspect of his schedule. My anger towards women getting pregnant naturally only increased. A female colleague at work had been discussing with a group of women how best to have babies and retain your career status. "Plan your pregnancies to deliver in the summer; it's that easy," she stated naively, "that way you only miss work when it's slow, and people barely realize you're gone." I wanted to slap her for being so clueless. It was the beginning of the downward slide in my career associated with the time demands of trying to and eventually having a family.

"Honey, something's wrong." I woke Brooks at 2 am one day. We went into the bathroom to get a better view. My entire back, legs, and arms were covered in hives. It looked like I'd been whipped, and the marks from the whip had swelled up, appearing as bruises all over my body. It itched like nothing had ever itched before. I couldn't help but scratch, which only made it worse. "I can't take it. What do you think it is?" I complained. We spent the next six hours at the emergency room, trying to figure out what type of allergic reaction I was having. No one suspected that it was from the heavy doses of hormones I was injecting my body with. There was nothing I could do; I would spend months covered in hives while limping and in pain in our efforts to have a baby.

After enduring several months of daily injections, muscle soreness, chronic pain, and hives all over my body, our first cycle of IVF failed. I had ceased caring about the meetings at work I was incessantly missing. My bosses knew something strange was going on, but didn't dare ask. I had been the model employee, always working and always available; I now only went through the motions, coming in late and leaving early, barely able to get my daily job done. IVF and my desire to be a mom had consumed all of my energy; it would be a vicious cycle I would never get out of.

———◡∿◡———

I dreaded starting another fertility cycle, but I knew I had to do it. It was our only option, and I couldn't give up. After the eggs were again implanted, and after I had already endured weeks of leg cramps and hives, I listened to every word the doctors recommended. "Try to remain as sedentary as you can," they advised. I took a week off from work to lie on the couch; the damage had already been done to my career, what would taking off another week do?

After returning to work, I still had to wait another week for the pregnancy test. I couldn't eat or sleep; I went to work, but was unable to talk to anyone. All I could think about was whether or not it had worked. I knew I had done everything I could this time; if it didn't work, I didn't think I could endure another IVF cycle. We would have to resort to adoption, but I wasn't ready.

When we went in for the ultrasound, the doctor looked puzzled as he moved the wand over my belly. "Congratulations," he said. "You look to be carrying two healthy babies."

Brooks and I looked at each other in disbelief, unable to even speak for a minute. "Two?" He finally said.

"Two?" I asked. "Are you sure?"

"Yes, look here." He pointed at two dots on the screen. They were only dots, but you could distinctively see them both. I wanted to jump up and down; I was so excited. Brooks' face turned white. I paid no attention as the doctors discussed the risks inherent in carrying twins, particularly for someone with my build. I naively assumed that since I was now pregnant, the rest was easy and inevitable.

When I sent my dad the ultrasound picture he named the two dots speck and fleck. Speck and Fleck would eventually become Kyle and Ashley; we knew we had no other names to consider. I coasted through the pregnancy, radiating in anticipation the entire nine months. I worked hours and hours to prepare for their entrance into the world. I painted Care Bear murals in the area that would eventually become their playroom in the basement. It was during the seventh month of the pregnancy, and probably not the wisest activity. But I researched the various types of paint to ensure I didn't inhale fumes of anything that could be dangerous. Each of the two murals I painted took five hours; I spent all night working on the one, and then completed the next the following day. Although my wrists and hands were sore for weeks from the steady grip I had to hold, the effort was worth it; the murals turned out perfectly. I would eventually paint many pictures for them over the years, valuing the joy and appreciation they acquired for my creative gifts.

---

My dad never talked about my sister who had died, Alexandra, and I didn't feel comfortable asking. As a two year old, I didn't have any recollection of losing a sibling. But my parents had lost a one year old; I was now realizing how many memories could be created in a short year. All my dad ever told me was that she had contracted a fatal virus, and there was nothing the doctors could do in Vietnam. I wondered whether hospitals in the U.S. could have helped her. I wondered how long she was sick for. Was it sudden? Did she contract it at only several months old and then remain sick until she died at a year old? We had only several photo albums from our days in Vietnam, but no pictures of Alexandra. It was as though she never existed.

If it weren't for her name written in the Mother Goose book, I would almost question whether she truly existed.

I would wonder my whole life how I might have been different if I had a sister a year younger than me. I was always jealous of friends who had close siblings; I would watch longingly as they played and teased each other. Although I had only been two when we lost Alexandra, I now realized that although I didn't remember her, her loss must have had a profound effect on me. Kyle and Ashley's bond was quickly forming as babies; at only several months old, I already couldn't imagine what it would be like to lose one of them. I couldn't imagine what it would do to them to lose the best friend they had from birth.

The dynamics of twins was fascinating to watch. We put Kyle and Ashley to sleep next to each other in the same crib. It wasn't long before they would cuddle up against each other, finding their preferred sleeping positions. Kyle was the more dominant one, even though he had been born slightly smaller, and was soon pushing Ashley into the corner of the crib. I thought of Alexandra and me. We had only been a year apart, and in our small apartment in Laos, we also shared a bed. I had been the more dominant one, partly by age, but also by personality. I was the Kyle in our sibling relationship. But just as I was old enough to legitimately exert my dominance over her, she was gone, leaving me to grow up as an only child. Kyle and Ashley would never experience the level of one on one attention I received from my dad. They would never know what it was like to be the sole pride and joy of a parent. But they would also never have to know how lonely it could be as an only child. They would both learn to fight for the limited attention Brooks and I were able to give to all of our children.

# Chapter 7 - Birthdays

My seventh birthday was celebrated in our new home. I finally had some friends to invite. Tommy, Jason, and I had become inseparable, and I had started to see Sammy again at the Laundromat. I also now had several girlfriends at school. I was bouncing off the walls in anticipation of the day. My dad said I could invite five of my friends over and he would bake a cake. I couldn't believe my dad was going to make a cake; wasn't that something only moms did?

I was old enough to understand that I didn't have a mother. For the most part, I was happy despite our meager circumstances, but I was embarrassed to only have a dad, and when people asked, I didn't know what to say.

"Why don't you have a mom?" Jason asked me one day.

"I'm not sure. I guess my mom and dad didn't get along." I was comfortable with Jason, but was hesitant to tell him more.

"But why didn't you stay with your mom? Most kids stay with their moms."

"Maybe my dad loved me more than my mom." I knew my dad loved me a lot, but I couldn't imagine that my mom couldn't love me just as much.

When I tried to ask my dad about my mom, he would

brush me off and change the subject. I still had the Mother Goose book with scribbles done by Alexandra and myself. It was the only link I had with my sister and my mother. Growing up, I would occasionally sneak into my dad's closets and look through the few photos he had. He would eventually pass his photo albums onto me, and when I was forced to part with them, it was like my mom and sister were gone forever.

"It's your special day kiddo, we can have a cake just this one time."

We spent the morning cleaning up the house. Sammy had never been over, and I was a little embarrassed for him to see our simple home, but I didn't want my dad to know of my hesitation. There was no real way to fix up the house, but I figured if it were at least clean, my friends wouldn't care.

We all raced up and down the street multiple times. Even though it was my birthday, I wasn't shy to suggest we have a competition to see who could run up the street the fastest. After I won every round of the race, we turned to hide and seek in the woods behind Sammy's house. Everyone was having a good time, and I had never been happier. This was the best birthday ever.

"Cake time!" My dad screamed from the house.

"Yeah!" We all ran to the porch. My dad had even tied several balloons onto the porch. It looked like a regular birthday party.

The cake was toppling over a bit, but other than that, looked like a traditional chocolate cake.

"Okay, blow!" My dad screamed as I blew as hard as I could onto all seven candles.

After cutting a slice of cake for everyone, my dad went back inside to leave us alone. As we bit into the cake, we all began to look at each other and giggle. It was the worst cake ever. The inside was all dry and caky, making it stick to your teeth.

My dad leaned his head out the door, "How's the cake kids?"

"Ummm, great," I lied for the group.

We looked at each other, trying to decide what to do. No one dared have a second bite of cake. I took the lead and scooped mine off the plate and under the porch, where my dad would be sure not to see it. Everyone followed, giggling in unison. I didn't get to have the birthday cake I was so excited about, but it was the best birthday ever, and all my friends seemed to think the yucky cake incident was funny.

"Bye, thanks for coming." I waved off our last guest, tired and happy from the party.

Just as I sat down, exhausted from the excitement, and all the running races, my dad came outside.

"Okay, now its time for your birthday present," My dad started to lead me to the back of the house.

"Present! I have a present too?" The day seemed to get better and better.

"Yep, just wait and see."

We walked down the stairs of the porch and around to the woods behind the house. Sitting behind our house was a tiny white cat with black spots.

"Happy Birthday," my dad exclaimed.

"Is the cat ours?" I squealed in delight.

"The cat is yours. All yours. You have to give her a name, and you have to take care of her all by yourself."

I was ecstatic. Everyone on the street had dogs, and I didn't care much for dogs, but cats were sweet and cuddly. A cat you could sleep with and hold in your arms. I scooped up my new best friend. She instantly purred when I began to pet her.

"Look, she likes me already." She began to meow - a loud piercing meow. I accidentally dropped her as I moved to cover my ears. "Do you think something's wrong with her?" I looked at my dad concerned.

"She's just meowing. That's what cats do."

I named my new friend Meow. Meow could meow like nobody's business. She meowed day and night. Jason thought it was the most annoying cat he'd ever seen. I loved her. It was her way of talking and boy was she talkative. I was going to be the best mommy to Meow.

"Hey kiddo how was that cake anyway?"

"Great," I said again, "everyone really liked it. Didn't you see? We ate it all."

"Hmmm, that's interesting. I realized after that I forgot both the eggs and the sugar. But I guess it turned out anyway." My dad seemed pleased that he had figured out a new way to make a cake. "I guess next time I make a cake I won't have to bother with either. That's good to know."

Oh well, I thought. The lie was worth it. My dad had worked hard to give me an amazing birthday. He had done his best in every way to play the role of both mom and dad, and although it was impossible for him to be two people, I realized even then that he was doing a good job. I wondered how important it was for a kid to have a mom and a dad. Wasn't love and everything else that went along with it all that mattered? So what if my dad couldn't make the best chocolate cake. He was as good as anyone could be in teaching me the values of hard work and discipline; he devoted everything he had into raising me. I wasn't about to spoil the joy he felt in giving me the best birthday ever.

———✻✻———

I spent weeks planning Kyle and Ashley's first birthday. I had been staying home on Fridays and had formed a network of mom friends in the area. I also had all my work friends with young kids, and Brooks had his work friends. We invited more than fifty people. Even though the twins were too young to have any understanding of what a birthday was, I spent hours looking for an entertainer. Should we have a musician? A clown? Perhaps a petting zoo? I settled on the musician, and interviewed several before picking one. I ordered cakes from

Baskin Robbins, selecting an appropriate girl themed cake for Ashley, and a boy themed cake for Kyle. I thought of making the cakes, but didn't want to risk having anything too simple. We were expecting around sixty kids, and I wanted to make sure to have a gift bag that was appropriate for each kid. It took several trips in and out of Target since I didn't have much room in the cart with Kyle in the front, and Ashley sitting in the basket; I pushed two carts at once, alternating letting one cart slide down the aisle unattended, while I pushed the other one to catch up. I accidentally bumped into a couple of people and got my share of dirty looks. I went down my list – boy, age 3, girl, age 2, boy, 6 months.... I selected something special for each child, checking off the list as I fitted each gift into the carts, making sure not to cram Ashley. When the carts were full, we went through check out, brought the stuff out to the car, and then went back in again for round 2. It took hours to wrap each gift and label them with each child's name. I wanted to give Kyle and Ashley the best birthday party ever.

The day was perfect – sunny and seventy-five degrees. Everyone came and was thoroughly impressed at what an event we put on. The singer successfully entertained all the children for her allotted forty-five minutes. Even though the party was mostly an adult party, I was proud of my efforts as a mom.

The pile of gifts was an awesome sight. I felt guilty that every guest had to bring two gifts – one for Kyle and one for Ashley. I had contemplated saying no gifts, but I was more eager than the twins to open presents, and I figured we could always use new items to add to our toy collection. Kyle received more than twenty trucks, including many duplicates. Ashley got dolls of all varieties – talking dolls, dolls that cried, dolls that peed. Neither of them seemed to care much, and before long, they were playing with the large box that Kyle's Breuder branded cement mixer came in. I left them to their activity, carrying all the new toys down to the basement to organize.

I wonder how I might have been different as a mom if I had had a role model those early years. Would she have thrown me these elaborate birthday parties if she had stayed in my life? Would she laugh at my overzealous efforts?   Many of the routines Brooks and I had already incorporated into our life came from his mom's traditions. I didn't have a mother in my life to teach me how to be a mom until Pearl came along when I was ten.

I knew very little about our escape from Vietnam and why my dad had chosen such drastic measures to leave his wife. My dad panicked when he found out my mother was locking me in a closet all day; he felt he had no choice but to abandon her. The loss of my sister, my mom's behavior, and our departure all happened within months.   The anguish of losing a child was more than my parent's marriage could handle; my mom, unable to deal with her depression, had wandered the streets all day, while I was left to cry myself asleep on the closet floor. My dad wanted to leave immediately, but he first had to wait for his engagement with The Associated Press to be fulfilled; he had to wait for the risks from the daily bombs and explosions to die down.   He was strategic and thoughtful in planning his escape, wanting to ensure that no one would see us leaving, and in particular, to ensure that she didn't follow us. He assumed she would be gone from our lives forever, and that we would be forever safe outside of Vietnam.

# Chapter 8 – Moving on, and the role of caretakers

"Under the table now!  Go." My dad grabbed my hand and we both fell to the floor, huddling together under our flimsy aluminum kitchen table.   I brought my knees up to my face and buried my head inside.

"When is it going to stop?  I'm scared." I leaned into my dad for comfort, hoping he could wish away the howling winds and pounding rain.   The storm was like nothing we'd ever seen in Redway.   It rained most of the spring in Northern California, but usually only lightly, often barely more than a mist.  It was always damp, and despite temperatures that rarely dropped below sixty degrees, it usually felt much colder.  Our first Spring in our new house I had cherished the comforts of being inside; I had always dreaded the spring rains in both our packing crate and lean-to.

We could hear tree trunks cracking outside, and occasionally, the sudden and loud echo of a tree falling to the ground miles away.   Fortunately, our neighborhood had very few trees, but the Redway trees that gave our town it's name were hundreds of feet high, and many were old and weak, vulnerable to the strong winds.

"Just hold tight kiddo, we're going to be okay." My dad shouted; I could barely hear him over the sounds of wind and rain. I was too scared to even lift my head; I started to convince myself our house was going to fall down. Then we'd have to move back outside again. I didn't want anything to happen to our house, and pleaded again with my dad to make the storm go away.

"Make it stop, please, please." I wanted to cry, but I was too scared to even shed any tears.

We huddled under the table for almost two hours before the winds finally died down, and the rain slowed to a steady drizzle. I gasped as we went out our front door to survey the damage. Our house had been surprisingly spared; many of the houses on our street had lost their front porches. Anything that had been left outside – bikes, lawnmowers, and chairs – had been broken into pieces and strewn all over the street. Neighbors slowly emerged from their homes, and started crying instantly on seeing the damage.

Once the rain had completely stopped, my dad and I took a walk into town. Most of the storefront signs were torn off and smashed into pieces on the ground. One house had an entire Redwood tree lying across it. The trunk of the tree was at least ten feet in diameter, and the tree had crushed through the roof, settling smack in the middle of the home. We didn't know who lived there, but I hoped they had gotten out safely. Not a single part of their home would survive, and it would take months before the tree was cut and moved away.

I realized how lucky we had been, and felt guilty that others had suffered so much. I wondered if the homeless men by the creek had survived. Were they able to take shelter somewhere before the winds really picked up? There was no way they would have been able to live through the entire storm outside. We walked back home, both somber, and thankful that we had been so lucky. I loved our new home more than ever, and decided that it had a lucky charm on it that helped it survive that day.

———∿∧∿———

We left California when I was eight. After spending six years living outside, and then the last year living in our small shack, my dad decided it was time to move on and get back to the working world.

I'm not sure what exactly inspired him to look for work again. Our years in California, despite the hardships of living outside, were happy and carefree. I was doing well at school, we were now living in a real house, and we had a good set of friends who would be forever loyal. My dad, despite his many intellectual pursuits, lacked the level of drive, and particular monetary drive that I had. He could be stubborn and opinionated, but he was a true individual, and didn't care what others thought. He would never be one to conform to the crowd, and as he got older, would become more and more separated from trends in American society. I always cared what others thought of me, and always strived to be a part of the latest trends and activities. Although he would always be a hard worker, and his intelligence and curiosity would bring him career success, he didn't care about being number one and making as much money as he could. He had sacrificed his career to take care of me when he believed it was the only option. Now that I was old enough to attend public school, and his value as a parent in staying home with me was less, it was time for my dad to gain back some of his individuality.

I was sad to say good-bye to my friends. Jason gave me a necklace and a picture of the two of us together.

"This is for you, so you don't forget me," he had tears in his eyes as he hugged me good-bye. "Yola, I bet you'll be famous one day," Jason said. "I know you'll be everything you want to be."

I started crying at Jason's words. I had shared everything with Jason. I was no longer ashamed of our house in front of Jason. I wasn't ashamed that my dad and I had to hitchhike every month to get our welfare check. Jason made it all seem insignificant. I felt proud around Jason. I told him that I wanted to make a million dollars, and he didn't even laugh at me.

Larry and Jean came down to the house to say good-bye. We hadn't seen them in a long time. Even though my dad had said we would visit them regularly, we had only seen them several times since moving. Their house was miles away from our house, and it wasn't practical. I began crying just at the sight of Jean. I forgot how special she'd been to me.

"Now you take care of this little girl," Jean said to my dad, "we've got high hopes for her."

Larry rarely said much; he simply bent down, and placed a small locket in my hand, and then folded my hand up. "This is from me and Jean, something to wear around your neck so that you can look fancy whenever you want."

I liked Jason's parents, and since we were always together, had gotten to know his mom well. But I missed having Jean in my everyday life; she'd been like my mother. I usually didn't care, but Jean's hug made me wonder what it would be like with a mom around.

Our last good bye was to my dad's red and black checked shirt. We sat outside our house and my dad built a fire in the dirt. I hated the shirt he had worn every day for the past six years. But now that we were saying good-bye to it, I realized it meant the end of our carefree life in California.

"Okay kiddo, let's step it up." He had said the same words when we were preparing to move into our lean-to. But this time we were at the airport, in the international area. "Our flight will be boarding in thirty minutes, let's go," my dad repeated.

We each had a duffle bag. There wasn't much worth taking.

All that I packed was every dress Jean had ever made, and some other odds and ends.

We brought Meow to the local cat shelter; I was distraught and didn't understand why we couldn't bring Meow with us.

"But why?" I had asked my dad over and over why Meow couldn't come on the plane. My dad hadn't even told me yet where we were going, and I had never been on a plane before. I didn't understand why we had to leave Meow in California.

"Kiddo, don't ask me again. This is the best thing for her, and you can get another cat someday.

"But there will never be a cat like Meow. How can you say that?"

"Kiddo, I said enough. Now don't make me hear about it again."

That was it. I kissed Meow all over as many times as I could, barely listening as the people at the shelter told me she would be in good hands. Meow was my baby.

The worst part was that Meow had given birth to a litter of ten the previous week. My dad took care of the litter. He let me watch as he tied up all ten cats in a burlap bag.

"You might not want to watch this kiddo," he said. "But it's the best way for these kittens."

He dragged the burlap bag down to the river; I trailed behind, not wanting to follow him, but unable to stop myself. When we got to the edge he added a bunch of rocks to the bag and then tied it up. I started to cry as he walked toward the deep side of the river.

"How can you do this? How can you?" I pulled on his shirtsleeve, begging him to reconsider.

"Kiddo, remember what I said, this is the best way for them." My dad wouldn't even look at me; turning away as he spoke.

I could hear the kittens squealing inside the bag. And then that was it. He tossed the bag into the river and they were gone. The image would stay in my mind forever.

Without Meow I felt a loss. Even though I knew she was

just a cat, she had given me comfort, always being there and not saying a word, other than her loud pitched meows. I hoped she would find a new home, someone who would take good care of her. I thought of Meow as we started to run through the airport. "We're almost to our gate kiddo, just down this last hall."

I hid my mood from my dad. He was excited for our new adventure, and I didn't want to upset him.

My dad had found a journalist position with the South China Morning Post in Hong Kong - he was offered the position of editor. My dad didn't tell me for quite a while, but one day he sat me down to explain that we were off for yet another adventure. Although he was excited for the opportunity to be the editor of one of the most prestigious newspapers in the world, it was not because of the financial rewards that he was eagerly anticipating his new position. It was for the adventure of traveling back overseas, and the thrill of learning and seeing new things. My dad's time sacrificing his career and work for my care was over; I was old enough to attend free public schooling all day, and my dad, with the vagabond still in him, needed a new adventure.

Hong Kong was nothing like peaceful upstate California. I learned quickly how to get around.

"Ay ya!" The large Cantonese man turned around to see who had poked him in the arm. It was my trick for getting through the crowds. We lived in Causeway Bay City - the second most densely populated city in the world. I had no concept of what crowded could mean before Hong Kong. Every square inch of every sidewalk was covered with people; everywhere you went was equivalent to a jam-packed New York City subway. As a barely four foot tall ten year old I found it next to impossible to walk down the street. I was pushed between mobs of people, unable to see a thing. I'd stare at the backs of shirts - green striped shirt, blue checked shirt, and white shirt − the colors all blended together. Then I figured out a trick. I walked the streets carrying a bent safety pin. To get through the crowds, I poked people in the arm; it was the perfect level for me. When the locals would turn around in astonishment and scream the generic expression, "Ay Ya," I'd dash by completely unnoticed.

Our lifestyle had been significantly upgraded. We rented an apartment in the busy downtown area of the city. Our unit was on the 30th floor. It was a tall skinny high rise, rising fifty or more floors into the skyline. Everything in Hong Kong was tall and narrow. Each apartment had a balcony, and every balcony was covered with clothes hung out to dry. From outside, the apartment building looked like one big clothes dryer, a colorful collection of apparel. The noise was deafening. At all hours of the day and night, you could hear the sound of cars honking. The pollution from the cars created a gray mist over the entire city. The pollution was so bad that our clothes, dried on the balcony, always had a distinct hue and odor to them, looking faded and smelling like gasoline.   Our apartment was clean but hospital like in character. Every wall was white, with white linoleum floors, white doors, and white cabinets. Although it was relatively small, it was much larger than our small house in California. The kitchen wasn't much larger than a closet, but it had an oversized family room, and I had my own bedroom, with my own door, and one bathroom for us to share.

My father and I spent all day at the main department store in the city, picking out furniture for our new home. Although he'd only begun working, the newspaper he was working at gave him an advance to buy furnishings. It was our first experience buying new furniture and household items, and I was ecstatic. I spotted a desk for my bedroom. It was more of a kitchen table, but I instantly fell in love with it. It was made of white linoleum, decorated with splashes of pink. The pink splashes were covered in glitter, and I convinced myself it looked like a sunset.

"Please, please," I cried. "It will be perfect for my room. Perfect for me to do my homework on." I explained to my dad how it looked like a sunset, and would be very inspiring for my studies. He was always particular about making sure I sat in a quiet place to do my homework; I figured I could easily convince him how much I needed the table. I knew what my dad's hot buttons were, and homework was top of the list. I was becoming smart and strategic in pushing his buttons.

He rolled his eyes at my sunset comment, "kiddo, you're being ridiculous. It doesn't look at all like a sunset. It looks like a tacky plastic table with pink splashes. It's the ugliest thing I've ever seen."

We argued back and forth. My dad was stubborn in his taste, and insisted that the table was too expensive anyway.

As we wandered through the store, finding other items to fill our new apartment, I started crying.

"Please, please, all I want is that table. If you get me that table, I won't ask for anything else." I was being ridiculous and I knew it, but I had never asked for anything, and all of a sudden, the table was the most important thing in the world to me. My dad had dragged me half way around the world, and we were now in a huge noisy city. I was enrolled in a British run school, with teachers that used rulers to whack children on their knuckles when they got an answer wrong. All I wanted was a table, and I wasn't going to give up until my dad gave in.

"I'm just going to sit here," I cried and sat down on the floor in front of the table, "It's all I want in the whole wide world." I was bawling now, creating a scene in the store.

"Kiddo, get up now. Cut the crap. You are embarrassing me, and I won't have it." He got his characteristic angry tone to his voice, with his cheeks growing increasingly red.

My dad had a loud voice. Even if he was talking one on one with someone, he always spoke as if he were giving a lecture. People were always asking him to tone it down. But when he got mad, he was especially loud. We now had a crowd of people watching us. I was sitting on the floor, bawling and begging for the table. My dad continued yelling at me to cut my bullshit and get myself together.

A store manager had come over, babbling words we were

unable to understand in Cantonese. It was obvious he was asking us to be quiet, but neither of us was willing to be the first to give in.

Forty minutes later we had ordered the table, along with the other items to furnish our apartment. Everything would be delivered the next day. I couldn't contain my excitement.

My dad was barely talking to me. "From now on, we will call that table the cry table. Damn it kiddo, I'm not proud of the behavior you exhibited back there."

My dad was mad, but I figured he would get over it, and it was worth it to me. I had my table. When we left Hong Kong two years later, I would cry again to say good-bye to my table. I always remembered the "cry table" as my first real possession.

—⁓⋀⋀⁓

I sat staring out at the water. My dad and I were having lunch at the piers, and he had befriended two Filipino women. My dad was never shy to engage a stranger in conversation; it was his skill as a reporter. He had a genuine interest in anyone with a unique life. I quickly grew bored of the conversation, and was daydreaming as he quizzed them about political affairs in the Philippines, and inquired about their residence in Hong Kong. It turned out many Philipinos came to Hong Kong in search of work. Opportunities were scarce in the Philippines, and Hong Kong was the closest main land with a large population of foreigners looking to employ house help.

We hired Perlita as our maid that day. She was offered free room and board, with a minimal stipend beyond that. Although a maid seemed to be a luxury reserved for the rich, my dad was making decent money, and almost all income classes could afford the very low rates paid to house help in Hong Kong. My dad tried to convince me I would love having Pearl around to help take care of me, but I only wanted my dad at home.

I hated Pearl right from the start. My whole life had been

alone with my father. Why would I want a foreign woman living with us? Pearl was in her thirties, nine years younger than my father, and very attractive. She had jet-black hair, nicely tanned skin, and a thin petite build. Although she was only our maid, I instantly felt she was trying to assume a motherly role, and I despised her for it. She even looked like she could be my mother. She spoke English fairly well, but with a strong Filipino accent and mixed up tenses. I tried my best to avoid any conversation with her.

"Did you finish?" Pearl came back into the family room to check that I was done with my breakfast.

"Yep," I muttered.

She walked over to the windowsill. "What this is Yola?"

I had decorated the windowsill with scrambled eggs and broken up pieces of toast – the entire contents of the breakfast she had just prepared. Pearl was a good cook, but I didn't want her making me breakfast. My dad was supposed to be making me breakfast. If he wasn't going to do it, then I wasn't going to eat breakfast.

"I don't know how that got there," I answered.

Pearl was shy and I already had the upper hand with her. She didn't say a word as she went into the kitchen to get paper towels to clean up my mess. She also never said a word to my dad, although I repeated this same routine every day for weeks.

I dashed out the door for school while Pearl was in the kitchen, avoiding any possibility of having to say good-bye. School was several blocks down the street, and I kept my safety pin always ready in my hand to make my way down the busy street.

Hong Kong was ruled by Britain, and I was enrolled in a British school. We had two uniforms that were alternated each day - a grey overall style dress with a pink shirt underneath, or a pink and white checked dress. We had to walk in lines everywhere we went, and sit and stand perfectly upright. The teachers dressed in uniforms as well, and any time a question was answered incorrectly, they stood ready with a ruler to whack your knuckles. My first class was handwriting. The school placed a high emphasis on handwriting, insisting every letter conform to a perfect shape. Printing was done just so, and the precise cursive style they demanded took me weeks to master. I suffered multiple whacks to my knuckles as a result. I didn't care much for the school system in Hong Kong, and came to dread each day at school.

Pearl was waiting at the door to greet me as soon as I got home. "How was your day?" She asked, trying to befriend me. Her jovial tone carried no evidence of any grudge from the morning's scrambled eggs incident.

"Fine," I mumbled, pushing past her into our apartment.

"I have snack ready," she tried again.

"No thanks, I have a lot of homework."

I brushed by her and shut the door to my room. My cry table was my favorite retreat. I settled at my desk, setting out the hours of homework that lay ahead of me. Each night I had at least three hours of homework; I didn't dare attempt less than a perfect job, for fear of the knuckle whacks. The school system in Hong Kong was so intense that it would take me several years after we returned to the United States before I learned something new.

My dad was working a lot of hours, and I missed our time together. He would still ask to see my homework each night, but he no longer helped me with it, and no longer challenged every answer. Although I had dreaded his endless questioning in California, I now missed it. Although Pearl had more or less assumed the role of nanny to me, she didn't have sufficient knowledge or command of the English language to help.

⌣∧∧⌣

I began the process of trying to find a nanny as soon as I found out I was pregnant. There were many different ways to go about it – newspaper ads, Internet sites, or the dozens of agencies that had recently sprouted up around Boston. Several Internet sites included childcare as one of their services – Sittercity.com, CraigsList.com – they were free, but the volume of listings was overwhelming. Newspaper ads seemed to be a thing of the past, and after a quick look through the paper, it was obvious that newspapers were a hopeless resource. Friends who had recently had children, and hired nannies, raved about the services the agencies offered. For a small fee of $3000, an agency compiled lists of prospective candidates, videotapes of interviews with them, and conducted all relevant background checks. The cost seemed a little ridiculous, but why would you look to save money when it came to the task of hiring someone to care for your children? I signed up with three different agencies, ensuring we didn't miss any potential candidates. The resumes came poring in. Twenty year olds, thirty year olds, sixty year old grandmothers, all with varying levels of experience. I talked to every friend I knew who had ever employed a nanny, asking them what the most important characteristic was in searching for a nanny. I searched the Internet for advice on how to interview, assembling a five-page list of questions: describe your relationship with your family, why do kids like you, what is your typical day with kids. My questionnaire was broken down into five sections, exhausting every aspect of a person's character, experience, and background. I similarly interviewed each candidate's references, with a separate list of questions. Friends would ask for my lists for years to come.

I didn't allow myself to stop and really think about the job we were considering. This was someone who would potentially live in our home, and take care of our children while we were twenty miles away in Boston all day. Additionally, we would often both be on business trips, and wanted to find a nanny who would be willing to stay overnight. My dad had never left me as a kid, and when he had returned to work after many years of spending every day with me, I had felt slighted and abandoned. Now here I was, looking for someone to watch my kids the vast majority of the time. But it was a natural part of achieving career success, and everyone did it; I rationalized my doubts. Our first nanny was a disaster. We had focused our entire efforts on finding someone who was ultimately flexible. My diligently prepared list of questions had gone out the door during the interview. I found myself returning to my hasty ways, and caught up in the emotional aspects of the process; I wasn't willing to be the hard-core interviewer I had intended to be. Brenda was always available, willing to work nights, weekends, and more or less twenty-four/seven if we needed her. I never thought to ask her why she liked to take care of children. I never thought to ask her what a typical day with the kids would be. We let her stay for just over a month; fortunately, the month when I was still home on maternity leave. She lacked any passion or affection towards the twins. I was now aware of the true difference between someone who views a nanny position as a job, and someone who views it as an opportunity to take part in the very important role of childrearing. I didn't understand these differences before the twins were born.

The nanny position is a paradox. It is a job where you invite someone to be a part of your family, while not actually wanting them to legitimately join your family. You want them to take care of your kids like their own, but you don't want your kids to see them as their real parents. You want someone who will dutifully follow any house rules you set, but also someone who will take initiative in creating appropriate new rules. You want someone who will happily fold your laundry and change the sheets, all the while taking care of kids and providing them with stimulation every minute of the day. It's one of the most important jobs anyone could ever have, and with pay levels that often approach that of professional careers, the marketplace clearly agrees.

We called the agency, told them of our horrible mistake, and asked for a second list of candidates. All the candidates were terrific in their willingness to work hard and be flexible. But I couldn't find someone that seemed to have a genuine interest in kids, or one where I would trust them to love our kids like their own.

Linda was different. She walked in, scooped up Kyle and Ashley in her arms, and started cooing to them. She made sounds that made them giggle instantly. She clicked her tongue, stimulating them to look directly into her eyes. She hardly seemed to care what the pay was, and she told us right away of her other responsibilities that limited her flexibility. But her ability to love our kids like her own was evident instantly. We hired Linda the next day; she was the nanny anyone would dream of.

I had no idea how much Linda would end up influencing our lives, or how dependent on her I would become. The relationship between working mother and nanny is like no other; all sense of business is lost in the employer/employee relationship. It wasn't long before I viewed Linda as my employer, trying to keep her as happy as I could. Conversations went from, "I need you to do this…" to "what can I do for you?"

---

I was starting to accept Pearl as my nanny. We started to mutually agree on the differences between a mom and a nanny, and she had ceased trying to be a mom. I was growing used to her good cooking and particular method of folding my shirts. If my dad was going to have to work all day, perhaps it wasn't so bad having someone cook and clean for me. She even changed the sheets on my bed every day, and I loved climbing into fresh smelling linens each night.

I lay in bed that night, unable to sleep. It was always stifling hot, and only the very wealthy had air conditioning in Hong Kong. Consequently, I spent many nights tossing and turning.

Sometimes I'd just give up and sit out on our balcony, watching the cars and people down below. Hong Kong never really went to sleep, and all hours of the night, crowds filled the streets. My dad would often send me to the liquor store down the block to buy his beer; as I sat on the balcony, I gazed down at the types who frequented the liquor store late at night. I knew most of them by name.

I heard moans from my dad's room. What was that I wondered? I tip toed back into the house, peering through the crack of his slightly ajar door. I quickly ran into my room. I couldn't believe what I had seen. Pearl was in his bed, lying on top of him. I didn't understand, but now I knew, Pearl wasn't just our maid. I didn't know what to think. I wanted to cry, but no tears came out. I wanted to barge into his room and yell at him, but I didn't have the guts. I would never tell him about what I saw.

The next morning, I pretended to not know what was going on; I decided I was going to make life worse for Pearl.

"I don't like eggs," I complained as Pearl set breakfast in front of me.

"Egg is what I make, so you have to eat it," she replied. Pearl had recently become more aggressive with my behavior.

"Well, I don't like eggs," with that, I picked up the plate of eggs and dumped it on the floor, "now don't ever make me eggs again."

I got up and went back into my room to pack my bag for school. As I walked out the door that day I heard Pearl crying in the kitchen. I felt a twinge of guilt, but not enough to willingly give up more of my dad's attention to Pearl.

That day when I got out of school, my dad was waiting in the parking lot for me. I ran up to him, excited for the surprise. My dad had only come to my school one or two times. After the years of him picking me up everyday in California, it had been strange and lonely to walk home alone.

"Hey Carl, what are you doing here?" I asked.

"I got out of work early, and figured I'd spend the time with my favorite daughter."

I smiled in excitement, taking his hand.

"Let's take a walk along the pier, it's a nice day." The pier was several blocks from school, and was a retreat from the busy sidewalks of the city. The platform that bordered the water was very wide, providing enough room for bikers, runners, skateboarders, and pedestrians. But even on the busiest days, it didn't compare to the densely packed sidewalks. I loved to go the long way home from school, walking along the pier as far as I could, before I had to turn back to reach our apartment. Even though the water was a murky shade of brown, it was still an oasis compared to the pollution filled city. Hong Kong was hot year round, and with high humidity as well, was an uncomfortable walking city. But the pier picked up some breeze, and I looked over at my dad as his hair flapped in the wind.

We walked in silence for ten minutes before my dad said anything. I was enjoying the company, and hadn't thought much of his silence.

"Sit down kiddo." He said as we got to the end of the pier. "Now what's going on?" He spoke in one of his stern, serious voices.

"What do you mean what's going on?" I looked at him curiously.

"You know what's going on. You're giving Pearl a very hard time for no reason."

I should have known this was coming. "I don't like her, that's all."

"For what possible goddam reason?"

He was mad, but I didn't know what to say.

"I just don't."

"Well, you better figure out a way to get used to her." That was it; that was all he said. The conversation was over, and my first day spending time alone with my dad had been spoiled.

My dad and I would never fully discuss his relationship with

Pearl and the impact it had on both of us. I was longing for a mom in my life, but wasn't yet willing to give up any of my dad at the same time. He was longing for a female partner in his life, but didn't know how to tell me this without making me feel slighted. He would later tell me how torn he felt; he wanted to be there for me, but also wanted to move on with his own life. He had sacrificed everything for my childhood; it was now time for him to refocus on himself and his needs. It would take me several years to fully appreciate his position.

Several months later Carl and Pearl were married. I would never forget the smile on my dad's face at the wedding. It was a small ceremony at City Hall, with only one other friend in attendance. We acted like it was a big festivity regardless, throwing rice at them, and acting out many traditional wedding practices. I startled myself at how happy I seemed to be. Even though I hadn't yet completely given up on my abuse of Pearl, seeing my dad so happy made all the difference. Was I ready to accept Pearl as my mom?

⌒‿ᴧᴧ‿⌒

Carl and Pearl's relationship didn't change much after their marriage. Pearl still did all the cleaning, laundry, and cooking. We put away Pearl's cot in the living room, and she officially moved her belongings into my dad's room. Pearl still made me breakfast, and I gave up on my protests of her efforts to cook for me. I let her do my laundry as well, but beyond that, I was independent and had slowly gotten used to life without my dad around all the time. I loved all the homework the school gave me, and didn't mind hanging out in my room all night.

Carl and Pearl were happy. My dad was clearly the dominant one, and more or less dictated what food was made, what we did on weekends, and what was purchased for the house. But Pearl didn't seem to mind, and the relationship worked for them.

Carl and Pearl often did separate things on the weekend; my

dad could spend hours exploring the city, or passing the time at a used bookstore; Pearl enjoyed staying home and tending to the house. I loved it when we went out as a family; sometimes we would take boat cruises from the waterfront, with stops to sample the exotic food made by the street vendors. My dad enjoyed wandering among the aisles of the smelly markets in the city. Hong Kong was known for its markets, and every day of the week, there was a different market featuring something new. Most of them were outdoor food vendors, selling chickens feet, brain, and many exotic things I could never identify. One trademark was the snake soup shop. It was partially outside, and the snakes were displayed in wire cages at the front of the store. The process was to select a snake that you wanted, and point it out to the store clerk; the clerk would then grab the snake by the throat from the cage, and toss it into a large pot of boiling water. My dad loved to go over to the snake soup store, just to watch people buying soup. While the snake wriggled furiously in the boiling water, trying to hold onto it's last bit of life; the clerk would begin to cut it into pieces. All wriggling would then stop, and once it was completely cut up, it was time to be dished out of the water, and into a soup bowl. Most people would slurp down the soup right there, chewing vigorously on the tough snake meat. I was horrified at the sight, and would beg not to have to go in the direction of the store.

"Seriously, I hate snakes, you don't understand." I pleaded again as I trailed five feet behind Carl and Pearl as they walked through the market.

"Oh, cut the crap kiddo. You don't have to eat it if you don't want to."

My dad had zero tolerance for complaining, and refused to believe that I was legitimately scared of snakes. But every time I would see the snakes, I would be up for the following several nights, visualizing the grotesque creatures being chopped into pieces. I had nightmares about snakes, dreaming of them crawling around me and under my clothes. My snake phobia would continue throughout my life; eventually, looking at snakes in books became too much for me.

One of Kyle and Ashley's favorite books became "Polar Bear, Polar Bear." The book was about different animals, and what other animals they saw. It had a sing songy rhyme to it – "Polar Bear, Polar Bear, what do you see? Elephant, Elephant, what do you see?" Each page had a picture of the different animals. I had to skip over the "Boa Constrictor, Boa Constrictor, what do you see?" page. They caught me several times, but eventually got used to it, and at a very young age, seemed to have a better appreciation of my phobia that my dad ever did.

"Hey Carl, maybe we do something else today." Pearl ventured.

Pearl also didn't want to go to the snake store, but she had no choice. Carl wanted brains for dinner, and the best brains at the market were right next to the snake place. My dad had acquired a taste for adventurous eating in Mexico; many of the locals survived on only live bugs. He grew a fondness for caterpillars while volunteering there. Hong Kong was yet another adventure for him; it was an opportunity to sample delicacies that were unique to Hong Kong. Pearl was equally aggressive, having grown up in poverty in the Philippines, and perhaps their most shared interest was sampling exotic foods.

"Enough ladies. We are going to the snake store, and then to buy brains next door. Now that's that." He glared at both of us. Even though our reasons were different for not wanting to go, I felt a bond with Pearl at that moment. We looked at each other, stifling a giggle. My dad would have become angry if we started laughing at his demands.

On the surface, Carl and Pearl seemed to have little in common. But something about their relationship, whether it was the common love of exotic foods, or interest in sightseeing and absorbing new cultures, made them a happy couple. Carl was the breadwinner, and rarely spoke about his job to Pearl. Pearl dutifully stayed home, tending to the housework and my needs. At dinner, my dad would ask me about school, but Pearl rarely said a word. After dinner, I would retreat to my room to do my homework; my dad would settle on a couch to read his book, and Pearl would putter in the kitchen. We might not have been the most traditional of families, but we were a happy family; my dad and I had come so far from our days in California.

# Chapter 9 – The role of a mother

"Get under the table now!" My dad screamed at Pearl and me, grabbing both of us as we all fell to the floor and huddled under our small kitchen table.

A burst of wind suddenly caused every window in our living room to smash into pieces, the million shards of glass scattering around the floor. Our table was twenty feet from the window, and only several pieces made it to where we were huddled. But now with the windows open, the rain began poring into our apartment. The wind was gusting so hard that the rain was coming down sideways, and the water came directly inside, soaking everything in our apartment instantly. Typhoons were common in Hong Kong, but it had been two years since the last bad one. I shuddered, now soaking wet and cold; in between gusts of wind, I could hear what sounded like people screaming from the streets down below. The apartment building swayed each time the wind blew; I began to fear that the entire building would topple over. I remembered the storm in Redway, and the house with the fallen redwood tree on it. At least there were no trees to fall in Hong Kong.

Once the rain stopped we crawled out from under the table, and spent the next three hours soaking all the water up off the floor. We used every paper towel and towel we had in the apartment, tossing our trash out onto the street as we soaked up one item after another. We literally picked up the rugs and tossed them out the window; they were damaged beyond repair, and no one would notice our garbage amongst all the debris. Looking out the window, you could see residents of neighboring apartment buildings doing the same thing. All the clothes that were typically hung out to dry on the balconies had blown off, except for a rare torn shirt that remain attached to a metal clothesline. I stood at the window, staring at the awesome sight below. The sidewalks were covered with broken up neon street signs, thousand and thousands of signs with the tiny bulbs that typically burned inside them ripped to shreds. I couldn't imagine how the city would ever clean up such a disastrous sight.

———∿∿———

We moved back to the States after two years in Hong Kong. It was ironic how we had left both California and Hong Kong right after a storm. My dad's father had become ill, and already somewhat antsy with the lifestyle in Hong Kong, my dad was eager for an excuse to move yet again.

We flew into New York City and spent several days with a friend of my dad's from the war before taking the train to upstate New York. New York City was an amazing sight. Pearl had never been anywhere other than the Philippines and Hong Kong, and had never experienced cold weather. We landed in New York in the dead of winter; it was a cold and blustery day our first day there. My dad showed us the Statue of Liberty, and the three of us had a blast racing each other up the stairs to the top. My dad had slowly acquired a gut during our time in Hong Kong, and the extra weight was starting to slow him down. He had bought Pearl an extra large blue down jacket at the airport, and she looked like a true foreigner all bundled up and still freezing while we stood and took pictures with our instant throw away camera. I would always remember the image of her, smiling with the wind whipping through her hair, while trying to keep the hood of her coat on.

We moved into the home where my dad was raised in Saratoga Springs, New York, with my grandmother and grandfather. I had never met them, my dad had never told me about them. I later learned that my dad didn't care much for his parents, in particular his father, an absolute tyrant, who berated his wife and everyone around him. I never understood the loyalty my dad felt in wanting to return home and help out his parents in their last years. My grandfather had kidney failure, and was hooked up at home to a dialysis machine. My grandmother, although still quite healthy, was unable to care for him on her own. It wasn't long before Pearl became the one who would change his urine bags, clean the tubing that connected into his bladder, and brush his hair. He was losing his sanity and would berate her while she did these things for him; it never phased Pearl.

Pearl had now become my traditional mom; she always made sure my clothes were clean, changed my sheets every other day, and took care to stock my favorite flavors of ice cream. She took a job for a while at Cudney's Dry Cleaners, but the pay was awful. Her face would break out from spending all day in a steamy back room. She turned to child-care as the only realistic means of making money for an immigrant woman in upstate New York. She started taking care of first two, then three, and pretty soon we had six young children in our house every day. It was chaos when I got home from school with all the kids crammed into our small apartment. Fortunately, I wasn't around much; with school, track practice, and on and off night waitressing at Friendly's; I was spending less and less time with my parents. My dad demanded, as much as possible, that I was home for dinner. We all sat at the table together for a good hour, and my dad would grill me on my homework and what I was learning in school. Pearl would sit quietly, never having much to say. Sometimes it was awkward. I watched as she dutifully served us and cleaned up after the meal, but soon I learned that this was her role. After dinner, she'd iron my dad's shirts and prepare his lunch for the next day. He took a brown bag lunch to work every day, and Pearl took great care in making sure he had a well-balanced healthy meal. My dad had become a decent cook after all our years alone together, but he never offered to help. He even had the guts to criticize her meals half the time. "Did you put garlic in here? I told you I hate garlic." Pearl was diligent and never complained. She seemed to enjoy playing the subservient wife, always there to help out when needed, but never exerting her opinion.

Every dollar that Pearl made she sent home to her family in the Philippines. As with everything else, she never complained. She saved all the clothes I grew out of, packed them up every several months in a large box, and mailed the package home to the village children. And every month, she would write a check, sending them almost everything she had made. I didn't understand this cultural expectation. She was viewed as the lucky one by her family; she had been rescued by an American, and was able to leave her village in the Philippines. Even though we had very little money, her family assumed everyone in the United States lived in luxury. And we did, compared to their lifestyles.

We visited Pearl's family in the Philippines one year. I hated it. I had to sleep on a hard concrete floor with a mosquito net draped over me in the hundred-degree heat. There was no running water, and the only way to bathe was to crouch in a walled in cement corner and dump a bucket of water over your head. I lost a lot of weight on the trip, subsisting on rice and bananas our two weeks there. Meals consisted of whatever animal they were able to kill that day. I had to watch the men chop up the animal, and then cook the meat over an open flame, making sure not to waste any of the parts. After the trip,

I began to understand that we were far more fortunate than I realized. I also gained a new appreciation for Pearl and how she had grown up. She had been raised in an environment far more challenging than our lean-to in California. Her tireless work ethic was a by-product of the life she had endured as a child. Pearl had probably grown up with not a single toy.

Although Pearl rarely asked me anything about my life, I knew she was interested, and would always be there for me if I needed her. She had an ability to sense when I was upset about something, and although she never said anything, her simple gestures always made me feel better. After losing my real mom for what I assumed would be forever, I felt fortunate to have Pearl in my life. I would sometimes wonder what it would be like to have a real mom like the type I always envisioned. The mom who would know all my friends, bake brownies for the school committee meetings, and sit down with me every night to help me with me with my homework. My dad had always done his best to be both a mom and dad to me, but our lives had been so non-traditional, that I never had the experiences some of my friends had. A part of me would always be jealous of much of what my friends had, but I was already seeing friends with divorced parents, parents who fought all the time, and parents who were never around. I felt fortunate to have the stability Pearl provided, and I was not at all remorseful for the permanent loss of my real mom.

Friends would often inquire about my real mom whenever they found out Pearl was my stepmother. I often didn't even tell people, and most people assumed Pearl was my real mother. Her Asian features were similar enough to mine, and we shared many characteristics. When people would ask what happened to my real mom, whether I kept in touch with her, and if I wondered how she was doing, I was almost embarrassed to tell them how little I cared.

I was happy at the public school in Saratoga Springs. I finally felt accepted; a stark contrast from both California and

Hong Kong. I was one of the crowd, and began quickly making friends. I joined the basketball team, the volleyball team, and the running team. I was naturally athletic, and excelled at all of them. As an athlete, I was in the more popular crowd, and although I could still not afford designer clothes, no one looked down on me. School came naturally, especially after all I had learned in Hong Kong, and I easily got all A's. I was becoming a happy and well-adjusted fourth grader. No one ever would have known we'd come clear across the world and survived living outside for six years.

The house we lived in with my grandparents was the same one my dad had grown up in as a child. It was a beautiful old Victorian home in the nice area of town. The street was thickly lined with trees and had extra large sidewalks; every house on the street sat on over an acre of land. All the houses on the street were large Victorians with wrap around porches. Every porch had rocking chairs and hanging plants. I was proud to live on our street, eager to tell friends our address. Most of my friends didn't know that we lived in the garage apartment of the house. The house had been in our family for years. My grandparents had purchased it for five thousand dollars in the early 1900's. After their children had grown up they couldn't afford the maintenance expenses of such a large home and paid to have the house converted into apartments. They then moved to the top floor apartment and rented out the rest. When we moved back, my grandmother cleared out the area above the garage for us to move into. It was still quite nice compared to how we had lived in California, but I was embarrassed to show most of my friends our apartment. I had friends come over to our house, but always had an excuse why they couldn't come inside. I claimed it would be easier to play in the back yard, or walk into town. When I'd walk inside I'd enter through the front door, the door that provided access for all the tenants. Our garage apartment had its own entrance around back, but I'd avoid that entrance if anyone were watching me. Through the front entrance I could access our apartment through a back door that entered directly into my bedroom. When friends would drop me off at home they'd often comment on what a beautiful home I lived in. I'd proudly say thank you without making any reference to the fact that it was apartments. I spent many hours by myself in the front lobby - the living room of the original house. I'd imagine my dad reading his books in that lobby when he was a child.   I'd pretend we lived in the whole house.

I was dazing out the window in class, when I suddenly heard all my peers start to whisper. Two social workers and a police officer had walked into the classroom. Before I knew it, they were escorting me out of class.

"Follow us, it will be okay." The one police offer spoke.

I looked up at him, petrified, but dutifully walked along, with one police officer on each side of me. I couldn't imagine what I could have done; my mind was swirling, but I dared not obey.

They sat me down in a back room I never would have known existed, and the social workers took over.

"Don't worry, we know your parents abuse you. We will take care of you from now on. Just tell us what it is your parents do to you?"  I looked from one of the social workers to the other, in shock from what they were saying.   I almost wanted to laugh, it was so ridiculous, but was too scared, and they were clearly serious.

"It's not true.  I don't know what you're talking about." But I couldn't say anything more; I suddenly started crying and shaking, making their accusations look true.

"We know you're upset; please, do not worry, you are safe now." The woman repeated the same phrase over and over as I continued sobbing.

I've never seen my dad angrier when the policeman and social workers finally showed up at our house, holding me back a distance of ten feet while they informed my dad they were taking me into the care of the Department of Social Services.

"What the hell right do you have showing up here making false accusations?" He screamed, his face becoming the characteristic bright red it always does when he became angry.

I huddled in the background, still unable to control my tears, but also unable to help defend my dad.

"Who the hell do you think you are? You will pay a price for this." He continued.

It turned out the social workers had misread the complaint received from a neighbor on our street claiming abuse of a child. The child's description fit mine – age ten or twelve, petite, half Asian, dark hair and skin. The house color was correct – white with black trim. The street was correct – Madison Avenue. But the street number was wrong – they were off by a block. The social workers, in their haste, had mistaken me for a young girl who was indeed being abused down our street. My dad spent weeks trying to sue the Department of Social Services, but with no luck. In the end he resorted to asking for a letter of apology; he was similarly ignored. He eventually gave up, and we forgot about the incident, ultimately cracking jokes about the absurdities in our social systems.

I had assumed another mistake was occurring when they pulled me out of class a second time.

# Chapter 10 – Biological mother

I sat in my fourth grade math class staring out the window, bored by the elementary material they were teaching us. Two years in the Hong Kong school system had equaled four years of the U.S. school system; it would be a good year or so before I would learn something new. Two policemen came into the room and began whispering to the teacher. Everyone stopped what they were doing, scared into silence.

"What's going on? Who's in trouble?" Mumbled numerous students.

The teacher and the policeman, after several minutes, walked over to my desk. I almost burst out laughing; I couldn't believe it was happening again. How could another mix up happen with me? Mrs. Applegate, my teacher, spoke first, leaning over and whispering, "Your mother came from Vietnam, and she is here to see you."

I stared at her, not believing this could possibly be true. I hadn't seen or heard anything about my mother since we had left Vietnam. My father never spoke of her, and I knew better than to ask questions. I had blocked her entire existence from my mind, almost convincing myself she no longer existed. I was in shock, and with numb limbs obediently got up from my desk and followed the policemen out of the room.

I knew she was my mother when I saw her. I hadn't seen her since I was two, and had no idea what she looked like. But there was no question that the woman who stood in front of me was related. She shared some of my characteristics - dark hair and petite. But she was pure Vietnamese, while I was only half. She had more typical Asian features with slightly darker skin and smaller eyes. She was accompanied by a man and a woman, the couple I would soon learn was representing her. My mother didn't say a word.

The male lawyer spoke, "your mother has come to the United States to get you. She misses you very much, and loves you very much." The female lawyer stated in a matter of fact voice. "She would like to spend time to get to know you."

I looked at the lawyer while she spoke, but kept focusing on my mother. It was the strangest feeling to realize this was the woman who gave birth to me; a woman I didn't know at all. I knew nothing about the path she had taken to now be here in my High School. When had she left Vietnam? Did she live in the United States? Was she remarried? My mother still hadn't said a word; she only looked at me and smiled, a complete stranger who would come close to changing my life forever.

I left school early that day, not telling anyone as I wandered alone out of the building. School suddenly felt so comfortable; I wanted to crawl into the tall thin gray metal locker as I reluctantly removed my coat and backpack. I paused and stared at the pictures I had decorated the inside door with; it was the thing to do at school – tape cool pictures of your family so people could see them as they walked by. There was a picture of Carl, Pearl, and me hiking Bear Mountain. Pearl was supporting my feet as I hoisted myself up rungs that completed the ascent to the top. We had grown to love hiking as a family, and Carl and Pearl were already determined to hike all twenty-six peaks of the Adirondacks. Although I had a look of anguish on my face, scared of falling, I remembered the day perfectly; we were happy as a family, and loved the sense of accomplishment of making it to the top. Maybe I could just hide inside for a day, and my mom would go away, I didn't need a real mom now; it had been nine years of not knowing if my mother existed. I had given up on asking my dad about her; I had grown numb to the questions constantly posed by friends. "Where is your real mom? Wow, you don't even keep in touch with her?" The comments barely registered with me anymore. How could she do this to me? How could she interrupt the normal life we finally had?

Carl and Pearl were waiting by the front door when I finally returned home. I could see the image of Carl pacing back and forth in front of the door even before I reached the driveway. His hands were waving up and down; I could almost hear his voice bellowing out into the street. Pearl's red face and swollen eyes said it all. My dad couldn't even look at me as he shuffled his feet back and forth and motioned for me to sit down on the couch.

"Here, read these first, then we can talk." His tone of voice was one I didn't recognize as he handed me two newspaper articles. My hands started to shake as I looked down at the pictures of my mom and me plastered across the front page of The Saratogian and The Schenectady Gazette, the two newspapers read by almost everyone in town. A current photo of her was on the left, with a line in the middle, and a picture of me as a baby paired next to my recent class photo. All I could think of was how embarrassed I was going to be in front of my classmates. I cringed, thinking of the ubiquitous "Saratogian" mailboxes in front of every house in town; no one would miss our story. I wanted to run down the street and steal every paper I could. I would never recover from the shame; how could I go to school when I knew everyone would stare at me?

"Vietnamese mother returns to rescue her child," "Vietnamese mother loses her child 9 years ago and returns to find her." I tried to read as I wiped away the tears that had now started to flow, blurring the already too fine print. They told the same story, both making my dad sound like a villain. They discussed how my dad had kidnapped me and fled Vietnam, leaving my poor mother abandoned. The story claimed she had spent the last nine years searching for us, spending every penny she made on her search efforts. To anyone who read the articles, my dad sounded crazy and evil; it was impossible to not sympathize with my mom and the horrible situation she had been put in.

A local husband and wife lawyer team had found my mother through a distant connection of theirs in Vietnam. They were taken in by her story, and because we lived in their town, felt compelled to represent her. The newspaper articles were filled with rave press about the couple, and their generosity in taking her case on *pro-bono*.

"Now kiddo," after letting me read for several minutes, my dad sat down next to me on the couch and put one hand on each of my shoulders, "it's going to be okay; she's crazy and no one is going to take you away from us. We will get a good lawyer." He stared straight into my eyes, almost looking foreign to me for a second, and making me feel even more uncomfortable. "You just need to do what everyone tells you to do, and this will be over with before we all know it." He was stumbling over his words, something my overconfident dad never did. It was obvious he was just saying things to make me feel better. I was only eleven, but I had heard of horrible cases where kids were taken away from their parents. I knew the power of the biological mom, even one who hadn't been in her child's life for so many years

I stared at him, still bewildered by what was going on. It all seemed impossible to be true. Although my dad had never shared much with me about our departure and her abusive behavior, I had naively assumed she was out of my life forever. A part of me felt cheated by my dad. Perhaps he had not told me everything. I wanted to understand more, but I was too upset and scared to ask. I sensed that this was one of those times where I was not supposed to say anything; I could tell by my dad's tone of voice and facial expression that he didn't want to discuss it. I wandered to my room, alone to question everything about my life. Why were things never easy for me? I was tired of being the tough one, and wanted to have a normal life; one where we didn't always have to worry about money, and one where I could escape from my past forever. My money dreams would come true, but I would slowly learn that money wasn't the answer to everything. I wouldn't have believed anyone if they had told me I'd ultimately give up my success to relive my childhood. I couldn't imagine that I'd eventually be proud of my childhood. I cried myself to sleep, overwhelmed with shame.

The days and weeks ahead were spent in court, a trial that would go on for over a year. Every day, my dad would take my hand and escort me up the long concrete steps into the courthouse. I couldn't open the heavy wood exterior doors by myself. I had never been in a courthouse before; it was nothing like I had imagined. The hallways were cold and smelled like ammonia. The white walls and white tiled floors had changed to a hazy shade of gray, and the windows were so grimy that you couldn't see outside. The room we would spend every day in for over a year was all the way in the back of the building, requiring us to pass twenty other rooms, all occupied by various cases – domestic violence and divorce being the most common. I don't know why they left the doors to each room open, but it was impossible to not listen while I waited for our case to start. I had little understanding of the nature of the fights going on, but the whole experience was thoroughly depressing. The divorce court I would later spend time in was nothing like the run down Saratoga courthouse. Boston's waterfront courthouse had won architectural awards for its unique design; the walls and ceilings had been hand engraved and painted.   Despite the miserable circumstances under which I had been required to visit the building, I had been in awe of the calming interior. I had stared at the bowled in and hand painted ceiling and remembered the Saratoga courthouse ceiling with the chipped tiles that looked like it might cave in.

"How many days a year do you attend church?" The lawyer was addressing me. "You stated that religion has played a role in your family upbringing, so exactly how many times do you go to church?" I was remarkably nervous on the stand, and felt under enormous pressure to say the right thing. I don't know why I had mentioned religion and church, but had figured they'd like a family that went to church regularly. I was trying to do what my dad had said, "just do what everyone tells you to do," but I refused to not take a lead in controlling my own destiny. Ironically, I was just one year shy of the age where I could have legally chosen my own guardian. In New York, a 12 year old was viewed as mature enough to choose which parent they wanted to live with. If only the courts would take the time to evaluate each child's level of maturity. Our years in California had forced me to age well beyond my years.

I wanted to make sure I said the right answer. "Well, we don't go every Sunday, but we go somewhat regularly." I shifted again in the hard wooden chair. I could barely see over the stand, and wanted to keep my eyes on my dad for comfort.

"Okay, I asked you how many days a year do you attend church?" The lawyer stared at me, an expressionless face.

"I guess 100 or so," I answered.

"100? You said you don't go every Sunday, that you go somewhat regularly, and now you're telling me you go 100 times a year? Do you realize that's more than every Sunday?" He barked at me, scolding me for catching my lie.

I instantly realized my mistake, but it was too late. The lawyers spoke too quickly; I always felt that I said the wrong thing, and they were very skilled at twisting my words. My dad had taught me the words perjury and slander in his work as a journalist, and the terrible consequences bestowed upon people who lied. Had I just committed perjury? What would happen to me? I involuntarily slid down in my seat, tears starting to well up with the embarrassment and defeat I felt.

"You are dismissed." I looked up, startled, and still struggling from my mistake. "Please return to your seat." The judge was now staring at me, as I felt frozen to the seat and unable to move. I couldn't believe the lawyer wasn't asking anything about all that my dad did for me. He wasn't asking about how much my dad worked with me on my homework, or how Pearl made a gourmet meal every night. They were making Pearl out to be a prostitute my dad had hooked up with; I wanted to jump out of my seat and slap them for insulting Pearl, but I knew there was nothing I could say. I slowly got up and walked back to my seat, forcing myself to not glance in the direction of my mom.

My mind began to wander as I sat and listened to legal presentations by each side that I didn't understand. I started to regret so many things I had said to my dad recently. I still subconsciously missed aspects of our carefree days in California, when my dad was there for me every minute. In characteristic pre-teen ways, I had recently become more rebellious and critical of my dad.

"Yola, did you finish your homework yet?" I had started retreating to my room every night by myself, and once I was done with my homework, I would write in my journal or count my money. My dad started banging on my door, acting like there was a fire or something. "Let me in to take a look at it." He banged again.

"Leave me alone I said. It's all done, now give me some peace and quiet."

"Kiddo, please do not talk to me like that. Now let me take a look at your homework."

"I hate when you do this. Why can't you just leave me alone already?" I continued screaming through the locked door.

"Kiddo, I'm going to ask you one more time. You better open the door."

I knew I had no choice, but not before letting our yelling conversation go back and forth several more times, and not before I told him how much he drove me crazy. He stayed in my room for the next hour, reviewing every part of my homework, and quizzing me on parts that weren't even included.

What would I do if my dad could no longer bother me about my homework? I took it for granted, and never once let him know how much I appreciated it. I had never told him how much it meant to me that he didn't work in California. I didn't understand it at the time, but I now realized what a sacrifice he had made. I now had some understanding of how tough it must have been for him to raise a child by himself. They couldn't take him away from me, they just couldn't. I was completely helpless and didn't know what to do.

"I can't make any promises. As you know, the courts here strongly favor biological parents being with their children." Our lawyer, Nancy, had come over to our house to strategize with my dad. In our small apartment, it was impossible not to hear the whole conversation, and as much as I wanted to block it out, my curiosity wouldn't allow me to.

"But everything she did, how can that not mean anything? She's crazy, Yola can't go with her." I could tell my dad was doing everything to control his emotions and not yell. I cracked the door to my bedroom a little more, trying to see his face. His back was to me, and I could only see Nancy, sitting cross-legged with her arms folded tightly. My dad had been very happy with her representation, but he had no one else to take his frustrations out on, and it was obvious her patience was waning.

"You can't substantiate anything she did. It's just your word against hers, and she's very credible." Nancy continued arguing with him. After months of optimistic projections, Nancy's attitude had clearly become more desperate and negative. "You just have to let fate take its course" I heard her say many times. Even to an eleven year old it sounded ridiculous.

"But she's lying. Goddamit, don't you see that. Jesus Christ, we have to get our maid. We have to get her; she's our only hope."

My dad had spent hundreds of dollars on long-distance phone calls to track down the maid we had in Vietnam. It was the maid who had witnessed my mom locking me in a closet all day; the maid had seen how she treated me everyday. It took great courage and strength for the maid to even tell my dad, a cultural taboo for hired help in the country. After contacting almost every friend we had there, he had successfully tracked her down, but when they spoke, she had been unwilling to serve as a witness. She was a poor Vietnamese woman, and to her, the risk of speaking against a fellow citizen was tantamount to rebelling against your country.

"I wish I could make that happen, but you already told me she is unwilling to speak. Carl, please, you have to think rationally, we need a plan, and simply relying on your story versus hers is not going to make it happen. We need to get to the hearts of the jury members and make them see what an amazing father you've been." Nancy reached out her hand and placed it on my dad's shoulder. He was visibly shaking, and I involuntarily slammed the door to my room, startling them both. I couldn't bear to listen to any more of the conversation.

I didn't hear as many of the conversations my dad and Pearl were having in the middle of the night. The exhaustion of each day was impacting me more than I realized, and I was having trouble staying up much past dinnertime. The way my dad had fled Vietnam was wrong, even though he rightfully felt he had no other choice, and the courts frowned on anyone who broke rules. He and Pearl were preparing for the worst, and were strategizing about irrational ways to keep me. My dad was staying up throughout the night, crying and yelling at himself for being so foolish.

"Why do I always make these idiotic rash decisions? Goddamit!" I heard him yelling at Pearl one night.

"It's okay, it will be okay." I heard Pearl in between sobs. "We will make it work."

———ᴧᴧ———

"But I don't want to go." I complained. "Please don't make me."

"Kiddo, you have to. It will be fine. Just stay with Laura, and you don't even have to talk to her."

The judge had ordered me to spend every other weekend with my mom and her lawyer. The lawyer had a lake house an hour away, and each weekend she would pick me up first thing Saturday morning and bring me back home Sunday night. I was determined to not talk to my mom or her lawyer the entire weekend. I complained so much to my dad, that he was able to convince the lawyer to let me bring a friend along. My best friend Laura accompanied me almost every other weekend, and we did our best to make the most of it. Laura was and would always be a rock in my life. Her mother was divorced, but had a lot of money. They lived in a fancy house on the other side of town, and Laura had a sister two years younger. Her mom bought her and her sister a new wardrobe every season. Laura and I would laugh for hours as we played dress up, trying on all her new clothes and taking pictures of each other. Even though I was jealous that Laura had money and a younger sister, she never made me feel lesser than her. Her positive attitude and giggly personality brought us together; we were inseparable best friends. Fortunately, my mom was too timid to bother us much, and Laura and I spent the majority of each weekend hidden away in the room with the bunk beds.

"Why do you think your mom is doing this?" Laura was interested in the whole situation, and would ask me question after question that I couldn't answer. "It doesn't even seem like she wants to interact with you. I mean, she hasn't even said a word to us yet."

"Yeah, I know. It's weird I guess. But she's my mom, what am I supposed to do? Aren't moms always supposed to be there for you?" I paused to think about what I had just said. She hadn't been there for me at all, and if everything my dad had told me about her locking me in a closet all day was true, then she had really never been there. Just because she had given birth to me, what did that matter?

I would later learn how there was so much more to being a mom than just giving birth. Being a mom required you to give almost everything of yourself for your kids. Even if my mom was suffering from depression after my sister had died, it was her duty as a mom to stay strong and be there for me. She had failed to do that, and had taken the risk as a mother that she would suffer the consequences. Her attitude seemed almost nonchalant in how she was interacting with Laura and me. She smiled and looked at us, but was happy to let us do our own thing, perhaps assuming that the gifts her lawyer gave us each week would be enough for me to love her again. I loved the gifts, but they did nothing to endear me to her. She remained a stranger as far as I was concerned, and I felt no emotional attachment.

My mother's testimony came later on in the trial. She was clearly nervous as she took the stand.

Her lawyer began the questioning, "Please tell us about when Yolanda was born."

She spoke very softly; the entire courtroom hushed, straining to hear her answers. "We lived in Vietnam. It was during the war. It was a hard life. First there was Yolanda, and then her sister Alexandra a year later. I stay home while my husband go to work everyday. He work long hours and I by myself." She gained confidence as she told her story. "Alexandra got very sick. It was hard for us. We fight very much. I think he did not care. He told me it was my fault. But there was nothing we could do. The hospital could not save her." She paused as a tear rolled down her cheek. "One day I go out to the store. I come home and Carl and Yola are not there. Something not seem right. Clothes were gone. I wait and wait. Then I realize, they are gone." She now started to cry harder, stopping to take breaths to regain control. " I go to police several days later and tell them that my husband and daughter have leave me. But it is too late. The police look for weeks, but they are gone." She continued to wipe tears from her face, smearing her make up everywhere.

Her lawyer asked, "how long was it before you knew where they went?"

"It was many years. I stopped looking and trying to find out after several years. I need to find work to live and could not keep on looking."

"So how did you find them?" He asked.

"I move to the US two years ago. One of my cousins move here before me, and he help me get into the United States. When I here I look them up, and find out they are living only several hours from me in New York."

"Then what did you do?" "I called you and you agree to help me get my daughter back. My daughter who I lost so many years ago."

Her testimony was very powerful. Looking around the courtroom, there were many people crying.

It was a difficult transition for our lawyer. "What do you do for a living?" Our lawyer asked her.

"I am a waitress. Two different restaurants I am a waitress at."

"What are your hours?"

"I work from 9-5, and then from 8-2 am."

"And where do you live?"

"304 Fourth Avenue."

"Please describe your apartment."

"It is a studio. Very nice. I decorate with items from Vietnam."

"How large is the studio?"

"I don't know."

"But it is a studio, meaning it's only one room?"

"Yes, but it has a kitchen and a bathroom."

I glanced over at my dad, who was wiping tears from his eyes. I had never seen my dad cry, and would remember the image forever. I quickly looked away, not wanting him to see me. I began to strategize on my own plan, not knowing whatever plans my dad and Pearl had concocted. I decided I would run away to New York City. We had recently taken a school field trip to New York, and I knew it was big with plenty of opportunities for work. I was only in fourth grade, but maybe I could work at a restaurant and live on my own. I knew my thoughts were foolish, but I had to find a way to fight off the reality and fears that were now finally settling in. I couldn't leave my dad and Pearl; my dad and I had overcome so much to be where we were. I was finally content with the life we had; it wasn't fair, I couldn't give it up now. I would find a way out of this no matter what. I started daydreaming, the tool I always used when I wanted to escape reality. I thought back to the daydreams I had had in California of being rich, with my dad and I both having fancy things. I daydreamed of my success, forgetting about the trial and everything that might happen in between.

My parents put everyone they could think of on the stand. It made me realize what a great person my dad really was to see how many friends came out in support of him, traveling to give their testament to what a terrific father he was. Teachers spoke about what a well-adjusted and smart child I was, and my running coaches spoke of the discipline and motivation they already saw in me. "What does it mean to be a good mother or father?" One of our friends had begun their testimony with this phrase, and the question would always stay in my mind. I would later overanalyze what would define success as a parent – A happy kid? A healthy kid? Many people would have different answers to this question, but even then I realized that it was the values my dad instilled in me, a process that took weeks, months, and years of being there with me every day. Raising a child to grow up and be self-sufficient, while striving to find happiness and success, is no small feat. My dad had devoted so much of his life to raising the best child he possibly could. It just wasn't fair to take that away from someone midstream.

My mother's custody trial finally ended. The weeks between the end of the court proceedings and a final decision would forever be the longest weeks of my life. I continued to question everything, at times feeling anger and resentment towards my dad for the many rash decisions he had made in life. Wasn't it partly his fault that we got ourselves in this situation? But most of the time, I just felt an emptiness and fear that I was going to lose both Carl and Pearl. I had grown used to not having a biological mother in my life; I didn't think I could grow used to not having the parents that raised me and made me who I am. I could never imagine having children of my own, and living in fear that something could make them suddenly disappear.

"Call to order. Is the Jury ready to render their decision?"

We had prepared for the final day, waking at five a.m. for our nine a.m. appearance in court. I couldn't sleep the entire night, tossing and turning, wishing there was something I could do to make it all work out okay. I had heard Carl and Pearl whispering in their bedroom, but had lost my curiosity to eavesdrop on their conversation. I felt numb, and spent twenty minutes in the shower, trying to calm my throbbing joints. I had layed out the blue dress I planned to wear weeks in advance, as though it even mattered what I was wearing. But I would always remember the simple blue dress with the matching belt as the dress that represented the most critical day in my life.

"We are your honor."

My dad squeezed my hand as he stared straight ahead,

seemingly at nothing. I struggled to hold back the tears, grasping his fingers for my life.

"Full custody goes to the father, with every other weekend visitation rights granted to Ms. Strock." The lead juror read from a white scrap of paper in a monotone voice, and then quickly returned to his seat and sat down.

I started to process the words, taking time to realize that the trial was over and I was allowed to stay with my dad. The tears began to flow involuntarily as my dad hugged me in a way that he would never do again. I almost collapsed into him, the relief starting to pour out of me.

I then began to reflect on the new life that lay ahead for me – one with a mother and a stepmother. Although I had spent every weekend with my mother over the past year, I still barely knew her. But I would surely get to know her if I stayed with her every other weekend for the rest of my life. But I didn't want to go away on the weekends. My father worked all week, and our weekends were time for our family. Before I could think anymore, I realized my lawyer was up at the stand, whispering to the Judge.

The judge spoke, "Ms. Strock has decided to decline her rights to every other weekend custody."

That was it; that was all he said. That was to be the last time I saw my mother. She was in my life from birth to age two, and then again from age 11 to age 12, and probably never again.

My parents never spoke of what happened. I wondered about my mother from time to time; does she still live in New York? Is she still a waitress? I've seen her name in the phone book when I've traveled to New York. But my curiosity stopped there. I've never called her, never tried to learn more. I knew I would never know the true story of what happened in Vietnam, but I also knew that it didn't really matter. I felt fortunate to have a wonderful and loving family. I wished that someday my dad and I could talk about Vietnam, but I assumed that this would never happen.  I had learned valuable lessons about the meaning of the word mom that would forever stay with me.

# Part III

# Chapter 11 – Raising children; what do they really need?

I was both jealous and aghast walking into Melissa's basement. I looked away from her, realizing my eyes were popping out of the sockets as I surveyed the room. An entire floor devoted to the playroom, it was probably two thousand square feet. Every wall had built in shelves. Every shelf was filled with toys. Each shelf was neatly labeled – "trucks," "cars," "Legos," "electronic toys." They had more toys than our town toy store. They had every toy you could conceivably imagine, all for two children. I took a deep breath, breathing in the over sanitized air; their nanny was probably required to clean the room of germs several times daily. Melissa gave me the full-blown tour, opening up one hidden drawer after another along the walls. The drawers were made of cedar, and the pungent smell of cedar filled the room each time she would open a drawer.

Kyle and Ashley started running around in circles, they couldn't figure out what to look at first. I bent down to pick up the cheerios Ashley was trailing behind her as she twirled around in delight, giggling in her manner that almost sounded like she was crying. Kyle stepped on a cheerio before I could grab it, crushing it into hundreds of microscopic pieces.

"Take down the truck box!" Kyle screamed in delight. I signaled for Melissa's approval, and then began the toy room deconstruction process, taking down not one truck box, but eight different boxes all filled with trucks. Every type of truck you could imagine – cement trucks, fire trucks, ambulances. I noted that they were all Breuder brand trucks. I was slowly building up a knowledge base of what the nice toys were. Fischer Price and Hasbro were the junky pedestrian brands carried by Target and Walmart. Breuder was only found in the specialty toy stores. Anyone with nice toys had Melissa and Doug handcrafted wood toys; Melissa had a whole shelf filled with Melissa and Doug puzzles and musical instruments. Kyle and Ashley, or any kid for that matter, couldn't distinguish between the more expensive branded toys, but the parents could.

Melissa's house seemed to be perfect in every way, with every amenity you could ever want to make life at home easier with kids. Who knew you could hire an architect that specialized in creating kid friendly homes? We had built our house before having kids. The playroom in our basement was in the back corner behind the much more important work out room. To access it, you had to walk through the work out room, avoiding dangerous machines and loose dumb bells. From the kitchen, it was impossible to hear the kids when they were down there. Every aspect of the playroom didn't fit our lifestyle – it was too small for more than one kid, and it was too far away to possibly multi-task while watching the kids.

We spent two hours taking out almost every toy. The floor was covered in what looked like a burglar's remains after ransacking a house. Kyle and Ashley had never had so much fun. I sat talking with Melissa the entire time, enjoying the peace of the free babysitting afforded by the new toys. Melissa also had boy/girl twins – Matt and Audrey. Matt had trucks and every type of boy toy for Kyle to play with, and Audrey had all the Princess dress up clothes and a full variety of make-up for Ashley to sample. The four kids weren't even playing together; they were too engrossed in the endless variety of toys to rummage through.

My jealousy of Melissa's playroom seemed to not just be the conveniences; I sensed myself fearing that we weren't giving our kids a sufficient variety of toys to be stimulated by and to learn from. Melissa had a full shelf full of electronic toys. In general, I didn't agree with electronic toys; kids should learn basic games of pretend and imitation. Electronic toys took away from the basic building blocks of learning. But I saw her kids playing the games; they were games teaching the alphabet, games teaching the names of the states. I watched in amazement at her kids, perfectly reciting the alphabet and the sounds made by each letter. Kyle and Ashley didn't know the alphabet yet. Was I depriving them of what was needed to learn these days? The only luxury I had as a kid was taking books out of the library; electronic toys were never an option.

———〜〜〜———

As a kid, my favorite activity was going to the library. My dad loved to read, and was always into a new obsession that he had to learn everything about. Throughout my entire life, he would always have a pile of books he was in the middle of reading. He couldn't read just one book at once. His favorite books he would read over and over, sometimes more than ten times. I was allowed to take five library books out at a time, and would spend hours pondering which five books to check out. I loved wandering among the aisles, breathing in the smell of all the books, selecting one at random, just to see what it was. I would read the same book over and over, until I had all the words memorized, and then would proudly ask my dad to test me to see if I could get every word exactly right.

"Carl, what do you think of this book?"

I had switched to calling my dad Carl. It was supposedly because everyone around us called him Carl. Without a mom at home to call him dad, I had grown used to people addressing him as Carl, and it sounded weird for me to say dad. Kids at school looked at me funny to hear me say Carl, but I didn't care, there were many other things they looked at me funny for.

"Laura Ingalls Wilder? Come on kiddo, that's too elementary, how about this."

He picked up some large heavy book about the Civil War. I was 7 years old and my dad seemed to think I was twice my age. He was always making me read books that were too complicated for me, and way too boring. His new thing was making me write down words in each book that I didn't know the meaning of, look them up in a dictionary, and then write down the definition in a notebook. He would quiz me each night from the notebook, making me cite both definitions of words I had listed, as well as use them in sentences. He continued this practice until I went off to college. Although it drove me crazy after a while, the exercise would eventually be one that I most wanted to imitate as a parent. I would often think back to the court case, and how I had almost lost Carl's positive force in my life.

We left the library with our bags full of books. I couldn't wait to get back to start reading my first one. I realized that many of the other kids at school had televisions, and I too wished we could have a TV. But I realized this wasn't possible, and for me, books provided a place of escape and a way to imagine the many places I could travel to and things I could have as I got older. The library and books had always been my version of school, even from our days in Vietnam. Pre-school had never been an option. My dad had proudly said to friends many times, "Who needs pre-school? Why should there be a pre to school?"

———∿∿———

Kyle and Ashley had recently started pre-school at LEAP – Language Enrichment Arts Program.   When I had first heard of LEAP, I laughed at the seriousness of the name.  Language enrichment arts – what did that mean?  Did they do art projects around trying to teach children language?  How was language enriched when the kids were only just learning to speak?  The whole name evoked snobbery to me.  How about school for toddlers?  Just leave it at that.  But before I knew it, I was sucked in. I was sucked into the long waiting lists, the laborious processes to get one's child on a waiting list.  I did what everyone else did – I called and begged.  I claimed I had gifted children.  I claimed to have a life long interest in their highly prestigious school.  I endured hour after hour of orientations, listening to eager beaver parents ask their anal and overly specific questions about their individual child's special needs.  I sat quietly, partly embarrassed to be there at all, but knowing I had to go through with it.  I couldn't deprive Kyle and Ashley of both a grand playroom and the best pre-school in the area.  The LEAP school was housed in several beautiful buildings, an upper school for the older kids, and a lower school for the younger kids.  I toured the facility, impressed at the cleanliness and organization of the various rooms. At the orientation, one particular parent dominated the question and answer session, "What if my son has to go potty while you are outside on the playground.  How long will you make him wait?" "What if my son has a runny nose, can I still send him to school?" They were perfectly logical questions, but they seemed so frivolous and obvious to me.

I also visited several other pre-schools housed in the backs of churches.  Their facilities weren't nearly as nice.  The hallways were dark and dusty.  The layout of the rooms was illogical, requiring a toddler to walk down a long dark hallway just to get to the bathroom.  They didn't have fancy names like LEAP; they were required to take the name of the church providing them with their real estate – Hancock Church Nursery School, Pilgrim Nursery School, First Baptist School – there were more than a dozen in our town. I liked the more laid back nature of these schools; Kyle and Ashley would be less spoiled in their unglamorous surroundings. I applied to both LEAP, just in case, and a handful of the church schools. My mother in law discussed the differences between pre-school and day care with me, something I had yet to consider in the process. Wasn't it all just a place to play? "What is the curriculum there?" She would inquire after I'd give her the update on what place I had visited that day. My dad thought it was silly I was sending my two year olds to school already. "School? How can they have school for two year olds?" He would laugh, stressing the word school, elongating the "ool" for emphasis. But he refrained from giving me any advice, he knew better. My mother in law went on to explain that true pre-schools had curriculums and had limited hours. Day care centers were places for working parents to have their kids babysat. They were often open twelve hours a day, and therefore the teachers were burned out and couldn't possibly engage the kids in some sort of curriculum. Glancing at the brochures, it was obvious the church schools were all day care centers by her definition. My hours spent touring and meeting with the directors now appeared to be a big waste of time. She continued to ask me about LEAP, "So what is their curriculum? What method of teaching do they employ?"

I gave the only answer I could, "Language enrichments and arts program. They enrich language through arts."

After ten more minutes of discussion it wasn't clear that she was convinced. I only felt guiltier for wanting to send Kyle and Ashley to school at such a young age. But it would only be three mornings a week, and everyone else was doing it, how could I not?

After getting home from Melissa's, I worked on convincing Brooks we needed a larger playroom.

"It's just not practical." I argued. "We have such a large house, it's a shame to not give the kids more space."

"But they already have so many toys."

I couldn't try to argue that this wasn't true. I felt foolish trying to convince him that we needed more space, implying that we'd then need more toys to fill the extra space, but much of what we had seemed to be junk compared to many of the educational toys Melissa had. I had already jotted down a list of things I thought we needed after watching what Kyle and Ashley had played with there.

"It's not necessarily for more toys. It would just help if the playroom were closer to the kitchen so we could run upstairs if we need to while watching them. Plus, it's so cramped down there. I don't enjoy even being in that room with them."

Brooks didn't seem convinced, but relented, never one to stop me when I seemed set in my mind. Brooks had an uncanny ability to read me. I could never hide anything from him; whenever I was stressed or upset about something, he would sense it right away. "What's wrong?" He would say. I always started with my usual, "nothing." The conversation would inevitably continue along the same lines, with us going back and forth. "I can tell something is wrong, what is it?" "Nothing," I would repeat several more times. Eventually he would get it out of me, and then mock me for trying to hide it from him in the first place. When he knew something was important to me, he would stop whatever he was doing and give as much time as I needed to talk about it. It didn't matter how insignificant or how much he might disagree.

I started calling contractors that evening. I decided we'd take down a wall, doubling the allocated playroom space, and move the play space to just under the kitchen. I'd get to work tomorrow, re-sorting all the toys, and figuring out exactly what to add to our collection. I even googled educational toys for two year olds, and how to create efficient play spaces. We were going to give Kyle and Ashley the best play space possible to stimulate their development.

———\\\\———

Christmas was in two months, and I figured the space would be remodeled in plenty of time; I'd surprise the kids with the new toys to fill the extra space. I was trying to explain Santa Claus to them. They were a little young, and only ran away in tears on my first attempt to have them sit on Santa's lap at the mall.

"Guys, this is Santa Claus," we were at the mall the second time, "if you sit on his lap and tell him all the toys you want, he'll get them for you for Christmas."

Kyle started to take a step forward; his big brown eyes open wider than I'd ever seen them as he stared at the long white beard. Ashley continued her tight hold of my hand.

"There you go. That a boy!" Santa Claus bellowed as he reached out for Kyle's hand, bringing him closer to sit on his lap."

Kyle looked to me for approval as he took his hand with both hesitation and excitement. Ashley and I watched as Santa asked him what he should bring in his sled to our house for Christmas.

"A green garbage truck." Kyle whispered. I could barely hear him.

"What's that boy?"

"He said a green garbage truck." I offered.

"A green garbage truck! Now that's a great thing to want. Santa will be sure to bring you a really big one!"

At that, Kyle's whole face lit up, his eyes beaming with excitement. Bigger was always better to Kyle, and he was starting to buy into the Santa thing.

"And a dump truck. A really big dump truck." Kyle added.

This time Santa had no trouble hearing him. Kyle started listing off all types of trucks he wanted.

"Alright son, I think I have your list down. Now you be a good boy, and Santa will see if he can find all those trucks for you."

Kyle hopped of his lap in excitement, running into my arms.

"When's Christmas? When will I get my trucks? Will I get all of them? Can Santa carry so many to our house? How will he get inside our house?" He rambled off question after question.

I tried to cajole Ashley into taking a turn on Santa's lap, but she was still hesitant. I finally sat with her and got her to mumble, "I want Princess things. All Princess things." She was equally excited, but less verbal than Kyle in her display of it.

It was so tempting to get them everything they wanted. Most of the items they asked for were only five and ten dollar items. It would be easy to get them twenty gifts each; we had the money. But I knew I had to control myself, I didn't want them to think Santa would bring them a large bag of toys every single Christmas. I didn't want them to think they would just automatically get whatever they asked for. I knew they'd also get many toys from their grandparents. Carl and Pearl would most likely get them one or two small things each. But Carole and Fred would probably have bags of surprises; they also couldn't control themselves. Carole would incessantly lecture me on the risks of spoiling children. But then she'd ignore her own words and be the first to spoil her own children and grandchildren. I was just as guilty.

―⁓ᴧᴧ⁓―

The riverbank became our simple amusement park growing up. My dad and I would go as often as possible, finding numerous ways to amuse our selves.

"Here kiddo, try this one."

He handed me a shiny bright silver rock. It was thin and flat, just perfect for skipping. I tossed it out, excited to get as many skips as I could. Kerplunk. It fell straight into the water.

"Oh come on," he exclaimed, "how could you miss that one? Here, watch me, I'll show you how it's done."

He grabbed another flat rock from the side of the river and tossed it out, making it skip four times.

"Teach me, teach me." I proclaimed. "I want to do it just like that."

The area around the river was home to many homeless people. People who slept in tents, or exposed outside on blankets. Even though we had lived in a lean-to and a packing crate, they looked so dirty and much worse off to me. Many of them looked like they hadn't bathed in years, and the men all had long beards. With the use of Jean and Larry's house, I had always been well bathed, and for someone who had technically lived outside, always looked pretty clean. I would feel sorry for these people, and if my dad said it was okay, would share my lunch with them.

I handed the man my banana, tentative at first, but feeling comfort as my dad stood next to me without saying a word.

"Here, you can have it, it's okay."

I looked into his eyes, searching for clues of his background. Who was he? Why was he here? I had so many questions that I knew would never be asked. He turned away, muttering a thank you, and disappeared inside his tent. I squeezed my dad's hand, our signal that I needed him to mobilize my now paralyzed feet.

"It's okay Yola, let's go eat our lunch now."

I hesitated, wanting to know if he would emerge again, if he would thank me for my banana, if he would share his story.

I'm not sure why exactly, but I had taken a recent interest in homelessness in our area.    I wondered whether my interest was a subconscious effort to bring up my past, as had inevitably already occurred. Was I doing this selfishly, now that I was proud of all that I had come from?    Or did I simply want to help and give back to those who similarly faced tough situations in life?  I was co-chair of community service for The Lexington Pre-School PTA.  It was a moms' group in town, charged with organizing activities and events for pre-school age children.  It was my effort to get involved in the town and to meet fellow moms and their children.  One of our community service activities was an annual gift drive for a children's homeless shelter.    I would cull children's wish lists from the shelter's web site, matching volunteers with specific children, and charge them with purchasing an item off the child's wish list.  The volunteers were required to bring the unwrapped gift to my home by a specific deadline. I would fill up several carloads of gifts and drop them off at the shelter in Boston. This was my second year doing the project.  Last year Kyle and Ashley were oblivious to my efforts.  I stacked the toys in the dining room as they were delivered each day, and dropped them off by myself at the homeless shelter.  This year I wanted to use the project to teach Kyle and Ashley that not every child was fortunate enough to have much of what they had. The dining room was filling up fast as I had recruited over one hundred volunteers to buy toys. Everyday, as new toys were dropped off, Kyle and Ashley put me through the same exhausting exercise.

"I want it! I want it!  Mommy, can we open it?" They would shout in unison.

"Guys, what did I tell you. These toys aren't for us. They're for kids who don't have homes.  For kids who don't have toys." They clearly weren't getting it.

"Why do some kids have no toys?" Kyle stopped screaming and looked at me with a calm seriousness, suddenly confused as to why some child would have no toys.

"Because toys cost money, and not everyone has a lot of money. You have to work for money."

"Why don't they work and get money then?" He asked very logically.

"Guys, did you know that when mommy was a kid she didn't have any toys either?  Papang stayed home with me instead of working."

"What did you play with then?" Kyle again looked at me with a concerned innocence.

"I played with rocks, I made forts out of sticks.  I did lots of things."

"I want to make a fort out of sticks." Ashley chimed in, always eager to try any new activity.

"I want to play with rocks." Kyle added.

"We can do all of that.  I promise to show you how."  I was momentarily excited to think I could teach them some of the activities I had done as a child. Toys were always the easy solution, and the one I was growing accustomed to falling back on  – just buy a new toy – it was usually worth an hour of free babysitting to get other things done.

⌒⌐ᴧᴧᴧ⌐‿

After giving the homeless man my banana, we found a spot on the rocks by the riverbank. The rocks were damp from the rain showers the night before, and the whole area was wet and humid from the fog that had yet to lift that day. We didn't care, we were happy eating the peanut butter and jelly sandwiches my dad had made that morning, and the container, of course, of rice and beans.

"What are you learning in school this week?"

My dad awoke me from the daydream I was just settling into.

"Just stuff, you know, the usual."

I continued staring off into the dense cluster of trees beyond the riverbank, hoping he'd maybe settle into his own daydream. But not my dad, every meal we ate together was his opportunity to capture my full attention. An opportunity to grill me on school, words, math.

"Yola Strock, I hope you know what you will be learning this week. I hope you're prepared."

"I am, I am, don't worry." It's multiplication, and I can already do most of what's in our assigned chapters."

Bragging to my dad was always risky, but I couldn't help it. He always insisted I ask my teacher on Friday what we would be doing the following week, and then spend most of the weekend getting ahead.

"Okay, smartie, what's nine times seven?"

"63!" I exclaimed without hesitating.

"Five times six?"

"30!"

We continued, until we both collapsed in laughter. A group of the homeless men had ventured out of their area to hear what all the commotion was, and were standing a mere ten feet behind us, observing my militant dad. They clapped at my last correct answer, startling us to turn around; we hadn't even realized how loud we had been talking. The men were looking on, with a seemingly genuine interest in our conversation. There were probably ten men in total, all different shapes and sizes, but most with long beards and tattered clothing. They were dirty, but other than that, didn't have the stereotypical homeless appearance to them. It was the curiosity you could see in their eyes, and the mild mannered nature they possessed as a group; I wasn't the least bit scared. Even if my dad had not been with me, I don't think I would have felt intimidated by their presence. I saw the man I had given my banana to; he winked and quickly walked back to their area. The others followed behind him, all without a simple hello. I wondered what the men thought of us.

I stacked the toys in every corner of our minivan, quickly filling the trunk, the front seat, and the area under their feet. I let Kyle and Ashley each pick two toys that they could carry on their laps. I was hoping that at the shelter we could find the specific kids that the gifts they were holding were for, and they could meet them in person. I was also hoping that seeing the building where the homeless children lived would have some impact on them. Barely able to see out the back window, we set out for The Home For Little Wanderers in Boston. It was in a fairly bad area of town, an area that I wasn't familiar with, but I trusted our handy car navigation system to get us there.

"When are we gonna be there? Where are the kids with no home? " Kyle and Ashley were fidgety. We'd been lost for over an hour and a half now. It was rush hour, dark, and raining.

I gripped the steering wheel harder. I was thoroughly frustrated, and sweating from the stress. I couldn't turn back, but it was past six p.m., the kids were starved, and I had no idea where we were. I turned on the air conditioning higher. The navigation system had seemingly sent us to a different Longwood Avenue. I had been to the shelter the previous year, and it was clear we were nowhere near the right area. The only thing that was clear was that we were in an even worse area of town. I was too scared to stop and ask for directions, and even too scared to stop at all, for fear that someone would see all the toys in the car and break in. I tried to dial the shelter again, but all I was getting was an answering machine. The office was probably closed. I climbed into the backseat at the red light, searching the seat pockets for a map. Isn't there supposed to be a map in here? Who took it out of the car? I had no one to be angry at, recalling that I had left it in the garage the last time I cleaned the car. The light was now green and a line of cars was honking at me. Jumping back into the drivers seat, I dialed the shelter again. Finally, someone answered.

"Home For Little Wanderers, how can I help you?" A cheery voice on the other end; it was probably an intern working over Christmas break.

"Listen, I'm trying to drop off over one hundred toys for the gift drive. I'm totally lost. I have two screaming kids in my car, and I don't know what to do." Kyle and Ashley started crying, sensing my state of panic.

"Where are you?" The friendly voice responded back.

"Well, that's the problem. I have no idea. We've been driving for over two hours, and my navigation system must have screwed up, because it was only supposed to take thirty minutes." I wasn't helping to find a solution, but I had to vent, and venting to an adult was more appealing than venting to two year olds.

"What street signs are you seeing? Do you see any stores?"

I tried to calm down, realizing she could maybe help. "There's no stores, it's all residential. Umm, I see Canal Street on the corner. Now Oak Street. I think I'm on Granger or something."

It took another ten minutes of driving and reading off street signs for the woman to recognize where I was.

"I think you're in Roxbury, not Dorchester; you're in the wrong town."

I almost started crying. How did the navigation system send me to the wrong town altogether? I clearly typed in Dorchester. I doubled checked to be sure. How could I turn around and drive now to Dorchester when the twins were thoroughly hungry and exhausted?

"Mommy, where are we? Where's the kids with no homes?"

I ignored their pleas, as I momentarily had the horrible thought of dumping all the toys on the street and turning back for home. I didn't even know which way home was.

"I have an idea." The woman interrupted my awful thought. "We have a small center in Roxbury. It's at 2 Main Street. I can call them and have you drop the toys off there instead."

I was disappointed. We wouldn't go to the main shelter. Kyle and Ashley wouldn't get to see it or meet the kids, but it was the only solution other than going back and trying again tomorrow. At this point, I just wanted to be done with the gift drive and my whole effort to teach them about the homeless.

We arrived safely at 2 Main Street several minutes later. I didn't even take the kids out of the car, as I quickly unloaded with the help of one of the workers. When we were almost done, I had the man helping me ask Kyle and Ashley to give him the gifts they were holding.

"Kyle and Ash, this man is going to take your gifts to the kids who will get them for Christmas. This man helps take care of them." I tried to explain, but was too tired for much of an explanation.

Kyle and Ashley, both wide eyed as they started at the large black man, agreeably handed him the gifts they were holding.

"Thank you very much. I will make sure they get your presents and will tell them they are from Kyle and Ashley."

Kyle and Ashley only stared at him, turning their heads to watch him turn and walk back inside.

We got home easily, five hours after we had left the house. Kyle and Ashley continued to ask why the homeless kids didn't have a mommy and who the man taking care of them was. They calmed down, now thoroughly exhausted, the point at which toddlers switch to a calm state versus the manic hyper state of overtiredness.

I was relieved to have our dining room clean again, and to have successfully delivered the gifts, even if it was to the remote location. Was there even a point in what I had done? Did Kyle and Ashley get it at all? I didn't really think so, but I had to make some effort to offset the over indulgences that I was increasingly guilty of.

Christmas at the Taylor family was a truly overwhelming experience.  Carl and Pearl still did very little for Christmas, and had long given up on getting any of us gifts.  My dad felt it was a waste of money, and it was impossible to get Pearl anything she would like.  I had grown used to, and didn't even mind, Christmas being an insignificant holiday.

The Taylors had twenty-five or thirty relatives over for Christmas.  My mother in law made the same traditional meal year after year – cold salmon, roast beef, spinach casserole, sautéed mushrooms, and mashed turnips.  Even the desserts never varied – apple pie, blueberry pie, pumpkin pie, and the awful plum pudding that no one liked except the one great uncle.  The whole house would fill up with the smell of plums baking in the oven all day.  At my parents' house, it was always a small crowd – just our immediate family.  My dad, adventurous when it came to food, insisted on anything but a traditional meal.  One year it was lobster, one year it was a sampling of exotic meats.  The first year Brooks and I were together we celebrated Christmas at the Taylor house.  The second year we celebrated with my parents.  Poor Brooks felt lost and alone at my parents' house.  It was truly boring compared to what he was used to.  He had even spent over an hour each day on the phone with his family, having the phone passed from relative to relative.  "Hi Uncle Craig, Merry Christmas.  No, it's just her parents here, a small group."  I had listened to him say the same thing over and over to every relative.  When we got home from my parents house we decided that Christmas every year would be at the Taylor home.  I told my parents we would visit them before or after Christmas, but that the actual Christmas day we would be away.  They might have been hurt, but they claimed to understand.

I was aghast the first year at the Taylors.  Both the living room and the family room had a Christmas tree.  Each tree was surrounded by gifts.  There were at least two hundred gifts between the two rooms.  I had never seen so many gifts at once in my life, even including the thirty-foot Christmas tree at the mall that was stacked with empty wrapped boxes. It was a beautiful and overwhelming sight. The tradition was to get very dressed up early on Christmas morning. I had underestimated what dressed up meant. I rose early, making sure to look nice in front of my new family, but when I came downstairs and saw Liesl and Tracy, both decked out in beautiful dresses, I quickly realized that the nice sweater and skirt I had selected was much too informal. Each child then had to walk down the long stairwell from the second floor to the first floor, waving to a camcorder held by my father in law, saying "Merry Christmas!" We spent from 8 a.m. until noon opening presents, then took an hour break for lunch, and resumed unwrapping until 3 p.m. It was literally exhausting. Brooks' mother got me eight different articles of clothing, a new salad bowl set, two framed pictures for our house, a selection of small vases to fill the small cubbies in our family room shelf, and a heart necklace with hearts representing each child. His sisters also got me several gifts each. And of course Brooks also gave me ten or so different gifts. Brooks' mom spent six months out of the year preparing for Christmas.

The relatives started poring in around 3 p.m. It was a refreshing and eclectic mix of people. While Brooks in many ways had the ideal Beaver Cleaver type of family, there was a large diversity in his group of relatives. A gay uncle, a drunk uncle, oddly mannered cousins. We again exchanged gifts with the relatives – personalized Santa Clause ornaments, mugs, stationery. Similar items seemed to be passed from person to person. My mother in law then broke out the song sheets. We spent the rest of the night singing out of tune Christmas carols.

———⌒⋏⋏⌒———

I remember the first year my dad decided we should celebrate Christmas. Jean and Larry said we could cut down any tree we wanted to on their land. They had over 30 acres, so there was plenty to choose from. We spent the entire day walking among the trees, inspecting each and every tree, as though we were picking out a fine piece of art.

"Why don't we get to pick a tree that actually looks like a Christmas tree?" I complained after several hours of looking.

"Why would we want a boring old Christmas tree?" my dad said with his usual sarcasm. "We want something that is going to be just ours, a tree that no one else will have."

We were down near the river, digging through fallen down trees and barren logs. Instead of a classic Christmas tree, my dad had it in his mind that we should find a large branch with as many arms as possible, and as smooth as possible. This was what was making our search impossible. Every branch that we found had been water logged, and many of the branches had fallen off.

"Here we go, this is it kiddo!" He proclaimed. "This is going to be our Christmas tree." He held up a large smooth brown branch. To me, it just looked like a branch.

"I guess, whatever you want."

I was now exhausted and wanted to get this whole expedition over with. But he wanted us to discuss why it was going to be the perfect tree.

"Look, we can get some tinsel and hang it all over the branches, we're going to have the best Christmas tree in California!"

It was a little hard to not get somewhat excited, since he was so excited. But I had begun to resent that everything about our life was different. I longed to have the comfort of a home like Sammy. I wanted to have toys, a TV, snacks and treats. Many of the stores in town had Christmas decorations out, and I wished we had a nice house to decorate.

When I got home from school the next day my dad had decorated the tree. He had covered all the branches in tinsel, and made a garland out of dried berries from the land. The berries threw off a pungent smell, making my mouth water for the taste of sweet cooked berries, the kind Jean would bake into her scones.

"Where are the gifts?" I said.

"Kiddo, we don't need gifts to be happy. Don't you have some school work to do today?"

My school had started giving homework, and I looked forward to each night completing my homework and showing it to my dad for approval. But I was disappointed. Sammy had told me about his Christmas, how he would go with his mom to the toy store and show her all the stuff he wanted for Christmas. And usually every Christmas he received many of the things he had asked for under the tree.

Sammy had explained to me one day. "You see, there's this man, and his name is Santa Clause." "My Mom and Dad talk to Santa Clause and tell him what I want for Christmas," he explained. "And, if I'm good, Santa Clause comes to our house on Christmas Eve and leaves presents for me."

This all seemed unbelievable to me. When I asked my dad why Santa Clause couldn't come to our house he only laughed and said that Sammy was making things up. But I didn't think Sammy would make up something like that, and I didn't trust my dad's answer.

The previous year my dad had given me a raggedy ann doll. I couldn't tell if it was new, or if my dad had bought it at the Salvation Army where we bought everything else, but it didn't matter. She had long red pigtails, a large smiling mouth, and big black eyes; I didn't care that her previously white skin was faded a hazy gray. I carried the doll everywhere. It was the first true toy that I had, and I loved it. One of the only pictures I've ever seen from my childhood was of me sitting on our front steps, holding my raggedy ann doll. Many images from my childhood eventually became a blur, but the raggedy ann doll I would forever be able to visualize perfectly. I had come to understand that we didn't have much, and it only made me very determined that one day I was going to have a different life. I'd dream while I walked to school each day of a life in a big house, filled with fancy things, and money to buy whatever I wanted. Sometimes my dreams felt so real that I'd smile as I walked, forgetting the realities of our life.

Christmas day came. Jean had made me a new dress, one just for the holidays. It was red, with a big white ribbon to tie around the waist. It was beautiful, and I couldn't wait to wear it to school when vacation was over.

The contractor took several days, creating the playroom I had long dreamed of. It was the playroom that I always wanted as a kid; my childhood dreams were slowing coming true and I was giving my kids so much of what I had longed for as a child. I spent all day making it just perfect.

Kyle and Ashley knew I was working down in the basement, but they didn't know what I was working on. When Brooks got home from work, I told him and the kids I had a surprise.

"Surprise, what kind of surprise? What did you get me?" Kyle was always quick to chime in, assuming any surprise was a gift for him.

"You guys have a new basement." I led them each by their hand down into the basement, with Brooks following.

"New basement! New toys!" Kyle and Ashley started jumping up and down in unison. Although I hadn't actually purchased many new toys, they were so excited with the new layout and accessibility of many of their things, that much of it appeared new to them. Our toy room still wasn't as good as Melissa's, but it was much better than it had been before, and I at least felt that it was as good as most of our friends.

I cleaned up around the kids as they started to take out toy after toy. Kyle emptied out the large bag of stuffed animals, sorting through, until he found his favorite – Jerry the giraffe.

He pushed aside the Raggedy Ann doll I had bought them when I was pregnant, stepping on it as he reached for a new Breuder truck.

# Chapter 12 – Career struggles beginning

We ended up spending most of every weekend in our new basement; Brooks and I enjoyed the spaciousness of the area as much as the kids. It was Sunday, and as usual I was sad, as it marked the end of the weekend. But this particular Sunday, I was unusually anxious, and was dreading Monday morning; I had to go to Florida for a several day conference. I had returned to an investment position after Kyle and Ashley were born, and was determined to get back on an upward career path. The new position I had been offered required me to reprove myself all over again, as work had clearly begun to doubt my commitment. The trip was only two nights away, but three nights for the kids, since I wouldn't return until after bedtime on the third night. I knew I had to do everything possible to survive and succeed, and I was determined to prove to everyone that I could do it; but leaving the kids to go away on business was difficult.

"Can you please just put the wash in the dryer?" I said, trying to not sound too sarcastic.

"All you have to do is ask." Brooks responded. Brooks was great at helping out around the house, but didn't always notice when things needed to be done. He'd happily put the wash in the dryer, empty the dishwasher, clean up the living room, but only when asked. Otherwise, why would you think to look if there were clothes that needed to be put in the washer? I was doing my usual Sunday night scramble. Do all the wash, lay out the clothes for the next week, cook the kids' meals for the week, and cook food for my husband while I was away. Everything I could possibly think of to make sure they could survive while I was gone. How could anyone function if I wasn't around?

We sat at the dinner table. 8:30 pm. Our typical dinnertime. It was impossible to get everything done any earlier than that; I insisted on a home cooked meal almost every night.

"We'll miss you this week," Brooks tried to make me feel better.

"Yeah," I responded flatly.

"Okay, let's talk about something else," he replied. He knew there was no point in trying to make me feel better when I had to travel. "At least you'll be able to sleep in, and go for a long run," he tried again to make me feel better.

"So how's your week?" I asked, trying to make conversation.

"Fine, the usual, just a lot of meetings in house." He said. Then he turned to our favorite topic. "Did you see Kyle building with those Legos?"

"I know, he's going to be an engineer I think." Our dinners were our only time to sit face to face and have a real conversation, one separate from the chaos of chasing after the twins, of constantly cleaning up toys, and preparing for the next day. I loved this time, but it was inevitably interrupted.

"Ma Ma," the kids called from their bedroom. Many of our dinners were spent listening to the twins on the monitor. I went running upstairs to see what was wrong.

—⌒⌒—

I had just landed in Florida. It was sunny, and seventy degrees. Okay, so I guess this isn't so bad. My meetings ended at 5 pm that day, and I started to think about the long run I would do along the water. I checked into the hotel and went to my first meeting. "We expect to double EBITDA in the next 5 years..........we believe we can take our market share from number 10 to number 5...........our margins......." I was fading in and out while listening to the presentation.

"Wow, that story sounded great," my colleague Mark leaned in and said to me.

"Yeah, it really did," I responded, trying to sound enthusiastic. The truth was that I'd been thinking about what the kids would be doing during the whole presentation. It was 3 pm; they were probably waking from their naps, getting ready for their afternoon activity. Our kids were spoiled. Both my nanny and I were busy bodies; the kids did both a morning and afternoon activity each day - the zoo, the playground, the water park, the pool. I had them in the swing at four months old. Linda was everything anyone would ever want in a nanny, treating the kids like her own. I put all that out of my mind, and raced into the next meeting room.

We were at the Ritz Carlton in Palm Beach. The meeting rooms were on the third floor, with a nice view of the ocean. My cell phone began ringing just as the CEO was being introduced.

"Sorry," I mumbled to the person next to me, reaching to turn the phone off. I glanced down and noticed my home number on the screen. I was about to turn it off, but at second thought, grabbed my bag and ran out of the room to answer the phone.

"Hey, it's me, don't worry..." Linda was on the other end. "Kyle has a temperature of 104." My heart sank. "He seems fine, but the fever is pretty high, so I thought you'd want to know."

I hung up the phone before she was finished talking, racing back to my bedroom to pack my bags. I didn't bother to tell my work colleagues I was leaving. I didn't explain to Linda why I had to be home for Kyle.

~⁓⌒⁓~

I ran through the airport.

"You don't understand, I need to get on the next flight out of here. My two year old twin is sick." I was screaming at the woman at the airline counter.

"Calm down Miss, we'll figure out a flight you can get on."

"Just get me on a flight, I don't care what it costs, I don't care what you have to do." I was a pretty nice person, and got along with most everyone. But when I was stressed, I had difficulty holding my temper. All I could think about was that I had to be the one to take Kyle to the doctor. Linda could do it, or Brooks could leave work early and take him. But I had to be there. I had taken both kids to every doctor appointment, and I wasn't going to miss one because of a business trip.

The plane ride lasted an eternity. I couldn't work; I couldn't read my book. I paced up and down the aisles, and chewed off three nails. I gripped the seat when we landed; why in the heck did it take them ten minutes to get the door open? What could be so complicated? The only seat they had was the last one by the bathroom. It took another twenty minutes to get off the plane. Why do people wait until the very last minute to get their bags down from the overhead? You'd think everyone would be ready to walk off by the time the doors were open. Some woman in front of me didn't even have her stuff packed up when it was her turn to move forward. I didn't want to be overly rude, so instead I sighed repeatedly for what seemed to be another ten minutes, waiting for her to put her newspapers back in her bag. One by one, she folded each paper individually. I sighed again.

Now she looked at me, "Sorry, I just don't want to forget

anything." She was nice and seemed genuinely sorry. I gave her a fake smile and sighed again.

I dashed out of the cab and ran into the house. "How's Kyle?" I said hurriedly as I burst in the door.

"Oh, he's fine now."

"Fine? Is his fever gone?"

"Oh yeah, it came and went. I called the doctor, and they said these fever spikes are going around, and that they tend to only happen once, and then go away."

I looked like a fool - standing there in the door, sweat pouring down my face.

"I thought you weren't supposed to be home until tomorrow?" Linda looked at me confused.

"Oh yeah, I just figured I'd end my trip a little early," I tried to say casually.

"Oh okay, well we're off to do baths, so see you in a bit."

I'd blown off the last 6 meetings, and now I stood there with nothing to do. Linda had everything under control. She always had everything under control. Even if there were ever a hint that things weren't in perfect control, Linda wouldn't let you know it. If I had attempted to give them a bath, a fight would have surely erupted in the tub; Linda would have had to come to my rescue, saying something typical like, "Oh wow, they never do that with me." Her comments always had a way of making me feel inferior.

"Sounds good, I have a ton of work to do, so I'll just go upstairs and finish up." I lied. I felt ashamed at my foolishness for rushing home unnecessarily. I was trying to be the best mom I could while working full time, but I often didn't know what to do and how to appropriately respond when needed.

⌒〜〜⌒

I knew I was reacting too quickly, but my hormones were already raging, and I panicked at the prospect of having three kids under the age of two. The doctors were just as surprised as we were when I called to tell them I was pregnant. "Perhaps it's a false positive, perhaps your body is still carrying excess amounts of HCG hormone from the twin pregnancy," the nurse had told me on the phone. Her explanation made perfect sense, the home pregnancy test was likely registering a false positive, and I had certainly missed periods before. I put it out of my mind and let another month go by, but still no period, and home test after home test registered a plus sign. I was eight weeks pregnant when my obstetrician finally saw me.

With the unexpectedness of the pregnancy, and my maternal instincts getting the best of me, I did what I usually do, and made a rash decision. "I'm pregnant. I know, it seems crazy, the twins are only six months old, but I think I should cut my schedule to part-time." I addressed my boss as though he were my best friend, the way I had naively approached work all along.

"Umm, wow. Well congratulations. That's great. What do you want to do?" Craig, the head of our department, was warm and friendly, uncharacteristic for a manager in such an intense business.

"I don't know, really, but there's just going to be too much going on at home, and I don't know if it makes sense for me to keep managing money. Maybe I could do it part-time, or maybe I could help out on the management team part-time." I was thinking out loud. I hadn't planned or thought through anything I was saying. "I know Cindy is still stretched, and I'm sure I could help her out in some way." Cindy was the head of the research department, and had been my direct boss for the past two years. She had been there for me during the IVF process, giving me all the flexibility I needed. She was a true friend, in addition to being a colleague and supervisor.

"Well, we could probably work something out. Are you sure that's what you want to do? You know, the second you want to come back and manage money, we will hold a position for you. You've earned it." Craig went on to reassure me that they valued my tenure and would do anything to keep me happy. He reassured me that I would in no way sacrifice my career by taking a break, stepping back, and working part-time for a while. We negotiated a two to three day a week schedule, and I walked out of his office feeling on top of the world, and proud of myself for acting on my instincts. Even if I hadn't thought through and analyzed what was best to do, it was working out, and I was going to be able to spend more time with Kyle and Ashley, and prepare for having a third child. I felt so lucky to work at Freedom, and have such understanding bosses. Cindy was thrilled to have me back on her team, and I knew I could trust Cindy and Craig to take care of me. I never would have foreseen how my perfect scenario could blow up on me in multiple ways.

I would later counsel many women on how best to navigate the business environment as a woman. Freedom's female percentage in the investment division was chronically low. But as much as we tried to tackle the problem while I was in management, it was impossible. It was a male dominated field and Freedom topped the list of companies in the business for their testosterone filled culture. I worked hard on my golf game, struggling to fit in and get invited to the social outings. I skipped my work-outs to join the guys for after work drinks. The exclusions weren't overt or necessarily obvious, but as a woman, it was impossible to not feel left out almost every day. The advice I began to impart, and the biggest regret I would have, was to leave your family life at home. I naively assumed that since we all spend so much time at work, why not openly share your personal dilemmas with your work colleagues, including your boss. As much as I realized my open-heart style was damaging my career, I found myself unable to change. I was too quick to act based on my current emotions, the way my dad had always done.

A senior male colleague had congratulated me on the birth of the twins after returning from maternity leave. Our five-minute conversation, and his unexpected invitation to discuss the conflicts I was already experiencing, would have a lasting influence on my career.

"Hey, congratulations. Twins, wow, that must be a lot of work."

"Thanks, it's great actually. They're awesome, and already on a schedule."

"Why don't you stay home with them? You know, my wife came back to work at first, but she's been home for eight years now, and loves it." Kevin began discussing the merits of one parent being home; how it was important for the development of children, and that perhaps I should consider taking a break. Although a part of me was shocked by the personal nature of his comments, I jumped at the opportunity to discuss the conflicting emotions I felt since becoming a parent. "I guess I do see myself staying home with them one day," I finally said. I didn't foresee that Kevin would ultimately be in a position to hold the statement against me.

It all happened on the same day. I was three weeks into my part-time position, enjoying the flexibility and comfort of the management job. Cindy trusted me to get my job done, and was happy to have me work two days in the office and one at home. On my day home, I would wake up early, work for several hours, and then spend the rest of the time with the kids. I had the perfect situation.

The technician at the doctor's office scanned the wand over my belly a second, third, and fourth time, a puzzled look on her face. I was oblivious to her concerns, and was getting irritated at how long the appointment was taking. I had already made a play date for the afternoon, and was eager to get on my way.

"I'm really sorry. There's no heartbeat." She was still looking at the monitor; I almost didn't realize she was talking to me.

"Excuse me. What did you say?" I jerked my head up, her words suddenly registering.

"I've gone over it several times, and it's confirmed; the heart beat has stopped." She repeated it again, still not wanting to look at me.

"But it was here two weeks ago. The heart was beating at 180. How could it just go away? Can't you try again?"

"I can't. I'm sorry. It happens sometimes. You will need to schedule a follow-up with your OB to discuss a DNC."

She handed me a towel to wipe up the goopy ultrasound gel, and then walked out. I lay alone in the dark room, shocked at what she had just told me. I hadn't even considered the possibility of a miscarriage. After the saga we had gone through to have Kyle and Ashley, I had naively assumed our challenge was in getting pregnant, not carrying a pregnancy to full-term. How could this have happened? What did I do wrong? I thought back to those glasses of wine I had had in the beginning of the pregnancy, before I knew I was pregnant. I thought back to the fifty-mile bike ride I had done.

I stumbled home, in a fog, and more depressed than I initially realized to lose the unexpected and happy surprise that had come our way. We hadn't even been discussing a third child, but now that we were no longer going to have one, I suddenly felt a void similar to the one I had felt when we weren't able to get pregnant the first time.

Fortunately, Linda was out with Kyle and Ashley when I got home; I wasn't up for interacting with anyone at the moment. I slowly walked into the kitchen, surveying the strewn toys all over the family room and into the kitchen area. The house always looked like a windstorm had been through. It was one of the many adjustments that came with being a parent that I was still getting used to; it was difficult for my organized and anal personality to deal with the natural chaos that came with kids. I sat down at the kitchen counter, and slumped over, laying my head down on the cold counter.

"Ugh, you've got to be kidding me." I said to myself. Seventy-five new email messages and four messages on my cell phone. I listened to the first message from my friend Denise at work, "check your email and call me if you want." The other three messages were all from her, saying the same thing. What could be going on? I hesitated, wanting to go up to our room and lie down in bed, but my curiosity was too strong.

There was a corporate announcement in my inbox, announcing that my two bosses, Cindy and Craig, were leaving their positions for other opportunities. Other opportunities usually meant they were leaving the company. How could they do this to me? We had just negotiated my unique part-time position only weeks ago. Now they were leaving; I was screwed. I almost collapsed on the floor, overwhelmed by the events of the day; I had lost my baby, and now I might lose my job as well.

# Chapter 13 – Winning and Losing

I spent the next two months going into work my regular two to three days, but with literally nothing to do. In an unexpected and dramatic corporate restructuring, Cindy and Craig had been fired from their positions. A new management team from the outside, individuals who knew nothing about my situation, had come in to shake up the culture. I had no idea who to go to or who to ask. I was no longer an analyst, a fund manager, or a people manager. I had been the random helper to two members of management who were now gone. I had taken a sixty-percent pay cut to take on the reduced role, and now no one knew who I was or what I did. I wondered how long would pass before anyone realized there was someone who occupied an office, took home a paycheck, and showed up for work, all with no job title.

I was developing a grudge, partially towards Brooks, for the downward spiral I had gotten myself into. Why was it assumed that I was the one who stayed home when Linda called in sick? Why was I the only one who left work for the kids' doctor appointments? Linda had been calling in sick on a regular basis, missing work close to once a week for a rotating number of reasons. It was impossible for me to continue skipping work at the rate I was without anyone noticing. I knew I wanted to be there when the kids were sick; I wanted to be the one to take them to every doctor's appointment. But Brooks didn't offer to help; it didn't bother him that he had only been to the pediatrician's once or twice.

Barry, the new director of our department, wandered into my office one day.

"I hear your good," he said casually as he sat down in the chair in front of my desk. He was cocky, but in a casual way. I had already read his profile on the corporate website. His profile was nothing like the homogeneous crowd that occupied our department – white males with undergrads from Ivy League schools and MBA's from one of the top five business schools, all of whom had worked three years in between college and business school in investment banking. More than eighty percent of the investment staff fit the exact profile. Barry had a PhD in philosophy; he spent his free time hiking and rafting, and was completely unassuming in his physical appearance. His tone of voice was soft and slow, not at all characteristic of someone who had excelled in business.

"Hi, nice to meet you." I responded, somewhat sarcastically.

"Yeah, you too. So are you in or out on my management team?" He quickly replied, seemingly unwilling to exchange any personal information.

"I'm part-time, so it depends what the offer is." I startled myself in my directness. Would I ever learn how to succeed in the business world? I was always too honest, and unwilling to give the false impression I was the ever committed and incessantly devoted employee I used to be. I told Barry right away about the twins and my miscarriage, as though any of it should be relevant to my employment. He only looked at me quizzically, clearly puzzled as to why I was sharing such deep personal information in our first meeting.

"I can handle some aspect of part-time, but no less than

four days a week. Here's my offer. I need someone to build a training program for the analysts, and people tell me you're the best person for the job. I don't think it's a four day a week job, but I'm willing to give it a try if you're as good as I hear. I have big visions, but I'll give it a shot with you. What do you think?"

"I'd need my salary to go back up if I'm going to take this on." What was I doing? Did I really want to work on building a training program? It sounded as far removed from investing as you could get. But what were my options? I wasn't ready to quit, and with no other job to fall back on, what choice did I have? I signed on, in Barry's words, to create a mini university within Freedom. I had no idea what was expected or how to go about it, but I was momentarily thrilled and motivated, listening to his grand plans. Perhaps it would be fun to learn something new and build something from scratch. My mind starting working in overdrive, planning in my head the steps I would take. My passion towards work was momentarily reignited in my entrepreneurial excitement. My competitive energy was briefly activated in wanting to create the best training program ever.

———

"Alright kiddo, put away the tears." I had just lost my first cross-country race and I was bawling in front of my teammates and my coaches. I was bawling so hard I couldn't ride back on the team bus. I insisted on leaving in my dad's car, and didn't even care that everyone was looking at me. I had been the top runner in the area. At age twelve I was winning every race against kids four and five years older. I had quickly become a running superstar, and even though running gave me less available hours to work and make money, I loved the fame. I'd already had my picture in the paper dozens of times, and had been featured on television several times. New coaches, the

Kranicks, had been recruited to the team the previous year, and they brought with them a crop of new recruits. The Kranicks were a husband and wife team – Art and Linda – they were both accomplished runners themselves, and had devoted their entire lives to creating successful athletes. They studied running as though it was a highly complex mathematic field. They trained our high school team like a top college team. Practice was seven days a week, two times a day. They monitored our diet. They monitored our sleep. Weekend practices took place at their house and were followed by a supervised lunch of pasta – one pound of pasta for each runner. Lunch was followed by an hour and a half stretching session. Part of training included required reading on running. Our running logs were reviewed weekly. Friday nights they called our homes to make sure we weren't out at the football games; they wanted us home resting for the next day's meet. Our team went from last in the league to first in the league; first in the league by such a wide margin that we had to leave the state to find relevant competition. Weekends were consumed with travel to neighboring states to compete in races. After we dominated the neighboring states we began flying to find competition. I went from number one on the team, and in the area, to number three. I couldn't take my downfall.

"Kiddo, get your act together now." My dad repeated.

"But I lost," I whined.

We were almost home and I still couldn't stop crying.

My dad glared at me, indicating he was done talking; his lack of words and facial expression were a powerful influence. It was the same facial expression he always used when he was disappointed in me. When he was mad, he screamed. He screamed when I had been inappropriate in begging for the cry table. He glared at me when I had cried saying good-bye to Jean and Larry. He believed I had to be tough no matter what, and crying was a show of weakness. My dad could be my biggest fan and biggest critic in the same day. He demanded perfection in everything I did; anything less than winning, or an A+ grade was not good enough. But when I did win and receive top grades, his praise was incessant, and meant the world to me. I would always strive to please my dad and live up to his standards.

My dad's lack of tolerance for crying forced me to bottle my emotions up inside, a character trait I would always hold onto. I never cried when my real mom came back into my life and threatened our family. I never let myself break down over Mike and the mess I had made of our marriage. Brooks, and the security I felt with him, allowed me to let go of my restraints, and I became much more emotional in our relationship.

"Well, do better next time." That was all he said. He didn't try to comfort me; he didn't comment that although I had come in third, my time was a personal best. He didn't rationalize that our team was now number one in the country, and I was one of the top runners nationwide. I could never quite understand my dad and his selected use of praise. But his strategy seemed to work; I was obsessed with winning no matter what.

I vowed to get back my standing as number one. My dad had always told me I could do whatever I set my mind to do, and I wanted to be the best. I knew my running would help me get into college, and I wasn't willing to sacrifice any chance I had of getting a scholarship. Even though our training schedule was already grueling, I started tacking on extra workouts whenever I could. I went running by myself late at night after track practice and work. I didn't tell my parents; they were asleep anyway, and would have disapproved of me being out at ten at night. There was a street that was exactly one mile long around the corner from our house, and I would go up and down it twice during my late night runs. I did the route so many times, that I had committed the layout of the street to memory. I could cite what color each house was along the way, and had the decorations of most of the front rooms memorized. I knew that number one was a yellow house, and their living room had a blue L shaped couch with white patterns on it. Number three was a brown house with grey trim, and their living room was all white with funky artwork on the walls. I would challenge myself to pass the time, turning my head and guessing the appearance of each house coming up.

Running had become my therapeutic outlet. I loved to run for the competition, and the fame that came from being a top runner. Many teammates ran only for the associated benefits of being a school athlete, but they dreaded practice each day. I not only loved practice, but I loved my late night runs, and every opportunity I had to run by myself. I had loved running as a kid, delivering my one hundred and fifty newspapers as fast as I could. I had used the time to daydream about everything I wanted to accomplish. Sometimes I would visualize myself winning the upcoming track meet; I could hear the crowds screaming, "Yola, Go Yola!" while I ran along, my bag of papers flapping against my hip as I dashed from house to house. Sometimes I would visualize years ahead into the future; I'd picture myself in a big fancy office, holding a top position at some company. Years later, when I learned Pearl had breast cancer, I went on a twenty-five mile run, unaware of how long I had been out. Running helped me manage the emotional stress during her radiation and multiple surgeries.

———∿∿———

I did what I always did in the new training role; I jumped right in, running before walking. I called every contact I had, and spent days at companies that had launched similar programs, taking in every aspect of what they had done. I wanted to copy the best aspects of each program out there, creating the ultimate university. I was unfamiliar with Barry's style and the expectations of the individuals he had populated his management team with. Freedom had always been a sink or swim type of culture, and my push ahead work style had been a big part of my success. I didn't realize that other ways existed to get a job done. It wasn't long before the human resources rep on our new team was scolding me for my approach.

"You did what?" Jim's tone of voice and demeaning look were instantly irritating.

"I spent the day at Goldman, learning everything about their program. I typed up the notes and thought you'd be interested."

"Yeah, I saw the notes. Interesting sure, but why in the world would you visit Goldman before putting together a business plan?"

A business plan? For an in-house training program? Was he kidding? I didn't know how to respond. My process seemed perfectly logical; what was wrong with doing research before acting?

Before I could assemble a response, he was waving his finger in my face with further accusations. "You should have sought my advice. I've been in HR for over twenty years. I can tell you how to approach this challenge." He stared at me coldly, as though I was a junior subordinate who had just botched the most important project of the year.

"I'm sorry, I guess I didn't understand that I was supposed to report to you." I tried to temper my sarcasm, but this was ridiculous. When did my job turn into an HR project?

I lasted eight months in the training role. Jim continued to criticize and berate me every step of the way. When I approached Barry for guidance and help in dealing with Jim's impossible style, I was blown off and ignored. I couldn't take it, and once again, with no thought to my actions, I told Barry I needed a new job.

Kevin, who I had naively opened up to after the twins were born, had been elevated to a role as one of the department heads. He had known me since my first days at Freedom; he only knew me as a hard working and committed employee. I approached Kevin, confident that he would help.

"Kevin, I want back in. I'm ready to work full-time again, and I can't be a part of this crazy new management team anymore." I knew Kevin was also frustrated with the new management team, and assumed he would instantly sympathize. Instead he awkwardly looked away, appearing distracted and uncomfortable.

"Ummm, you know what, I need to get to a meeting right now, but I'll get back to you. I'll have my assistant set up a meeting."

A week passed, and Kevin's assistant never called or emailed. I called, and she claimed Kevin never said to schedule a meeting. I left Kevin three voicemails before he eventually stopped by my office one day.

"Hey, how's it goin? How are your kids?" He said casually. I stupidly launched into stories about the twins latest development, unable to contain my passion. I loved sharing anecdotes of silly Kyle and Ashley incidents, always forgetting my advice to others to leave home life at home.

I finally returned to business, "So I think it's time for me to return to an investment role. I'm ready."

"Oh yeah, that. Let me get back to you."

Weeks again went by, with Kevin never getting back to me. I eventually went around him, approaching another department head. The response was similar. After ten minutes of small talk about the kids, a discussion I didn't initiate, I was again told, "I'll get back to you."

I would later realize that despite my anger and resentment, I was lucky that Freedom retained me at all. I would have five different job titles within three years of having children; not many other companies would have continued giving me yet another chance, even if it was in less senior roles. But regardless, I was again up half of each night, reliving the past several years. Things could have been so much different had we not had fertility issues. I could have plowed ahead at work, and now be in a position with enough seniority and flexibility to have the perfect career and family balance.  If only I had never switched to part-time upon getting pregnant so quickly.  Why couldn't I have waited to see the pregnancy through?  I blamed myself for reacting so quickly.

———∿∧∿———

After the miscarriage and the awful DNC process, I became pregnant again a short two months later.  It was just what I needed to ride out the horrible position I had gotten myself into at work, and I relished in the pregnancy as I quickly passed week ten, and began the second trimester. We were finally going to have a third baby, and maybe that was just what I needed to get up the guts to quit work.

The pregnancy came to a crashing end after five months of rekindled joys and hope; this time we had to purposely abort a baby who would unlikely live much past birth.  It was the first time I had seen Brooks cry, when the doctors informed us during our scheduled amniocentesis that something was wrong.

I had been observing the doctor scan the ultrasound wand over and over in the same area.  Brooks was busy checking his blackberry, assuming this was only a routine check up that he was asked to be at for morale support.  I was incessantly paranoid after our previous loss, and started to fear a problem.

"Is something wrong?"  I finally asked, startling Brooks to look up.

"There seems to be a heart defect," The doctor stated very matter of factly.  "An expert in this area will be in soon to continue the ultrasound."  With that the doctor simply put down the probe and walked out of the room. Brooks and I sat for a painful thirty minutes waiting for the expert to arrive.

"I'm really sorry to tell you," The supposed expert spent only several minutes passing the cold gooey wand over my belly.  A belly that was already big enough to warrant wearing all maternity clothes. All our friends knew I was pregnant; strangers had already started passing me on the street offering congratulatory words. "The nucal fold is such that we can be certain at this point that your baby has severe defects. That coupled with the heart defect indicates survival much past birth is very unlikely."

"What kind of heart defect?" I screamed out suddenly, interrupting the doctor as he was about to continue on. My mind was racing and I hadn't even realized I had processed his words.

"Impossible to tell at this point, but it's clear that it's severe enough, and even if we were to operate following birth, life expectancy would remain very low." His words sounded completely sterile and heartless.

He went on to advise us to consult a therapist, but that in the end, it was my choice to make. There was clearly no choice to make. The hospital wouldn't be able to perform the termination for four more weeks; I would be twenty-two weeks pregnant. The two other large hospitals in our area wouldn't perform second trimester abortions. We had no choice but to go to an abortion clinic; the lot in front of the clinic was littered with protestors. We entered through the unmarked door that they had described, using the code name assigned to us.

The memories of the abortion clinic and the wrenching pain I was in during the induced labor would stay with me forever. I took a three-week leave from work to mourn; I knew it would only damage my career further, but I was literally unable to get out of bed for the three weeks. I tried to be thankful for everything I had – two wonderful children, a great husband, and what in many ways was still a good job. I was thankful, but I wanted more; I wanted another child, and I wanted my career to return to its peak.

I became increasingly obsessed with a desire for a third child. The anger I felt towards others and jealousies I had towards those who were able to conceive easily were worse than before we had twins. It wasn't rationale, and I knew it, but I was unable to control my emotions. I wasn't sure of my reasons for being so obsessed with having a third. It was partially a result of the defeat I felt after the two miscarriages. It had become something else I had to win at, and so far I was failing, something I was unwilling to accept. It was perhaps a subconscious way out of my work situation. I would be able to justify leaving work if I had three kids; I didn't think I could justify it with only one or two kids. Plenty of mothers worked full-time with one or two kids, but I didn't know many who did with three young kids at home.

"Kiddo, you need to stop. You're going to hurt your body." My dad had become increasingly concerned with my health, and had turned to calling me more frequently.

"Don't worry, I'm fine." I lied, continually giving him the same excuses and explanations for why I would be fine.

Kevin eventually passed me off to a third department head who finally had the guts to tell me no. I would repeat the words he said so distinctly over and over in my head, "You've moved around a number of times; you need to reprove yourself before we can put you back in a senior role." I appreciated Dale's honestly, losing all respect towards Kevin, and his obvious bias against me, now that I was a mom. I was eventually offered a role in investments similar in seniority to the position I had held two years after joining Freedom. In partially acknowledging the significant step down, Freedom would allow me to work from home on Fridays. I would have to ask Linda to work five days a week again, but I knew I had to give the position a try. It was my only chance to redeem myself. I would work hard, and show everyone that my role as a mom would not impact my career. I briefly gave up hope of having a third child, and plowed my energies into work.

———∿∿———

I couldn't sleep all night, anxious for the meet the next day. Our team was in Buffalo, New York, staying at a Ramada Inn. We had traveled by bus, and the drive, which normally took six hours, had taken nine hours because of the heavy snowfall. There was a foot and a half of fresh snow on the ground, and the temperatures were expected to be exceptionally cold the next day. We had a team meeting after dinner, with our coaches handing out inch long spikes for the race. Our winter uniforms included tights and a micro thin turtleneck, as well as a set of polypropylene hat and mittens. That was all we were expected to wear; any additional clothing would weigh us down. It was the state championships, and dozens of teams had traveled to compete in Buffalo. Our team was the favorite, and this was my opportunity to stage a comeback. Many of the runners would break down in the cold and wind; I didn't know how my body would handle it, but I knew I wasn't willing to give in to any amount of pain. I visualized the course; even though it was impossible for us to do a trial run in the fresh snow, I remembered it quite vividly from last year. There was a large hill midway through the race; this was the point when many runners would slow down considerably. I was especially strong at hills, and thrived on courses with tough terrain. Our coaches spent hours with us doing hill repeats; we had to run up and down a several hundred meter long hill in the park twenty times each Tuesday. Hills were a core part of our workout routine, and I was especially strong for my petite build. I had less weight to carry up the hills, and I would fly by everyone heavier than I was on the inclines. I imagined myself in the race the next day, passing people as their gait slowed to a crawl on the tough hill. I smiled in the dark, excited for the meet. A team state championship was almost a given, but my standing had been variable recently; this was the opportunity to redeem my status as a top runner. I had to place in the top ten to get the invite to run in the national championships. College scouts came to watch the national championships, and there was no way I wasn't going to be there.

We awoke to snow gusting outside our windows, the noise of which made the windows shake. The base temperature was negative twenty degrees; the news said that with the wind chill it was negative forty degrees. The race was still on.

My teammates and I huddled by the door of the gymnasium. The start of the race was just twenty yards in front of the door; but because of the conditions, each race wasn't being let out until two minutes before start time. Girl's varsity would be the first race of the day, and consequently, we would have the extra challenge of having to trample down the fresh snow. It had stopped snowing in the middle of the night, but the foot and a half that had fallen during the day was more or less untouched. I could barely stand, trying to balance on my inch long spikes. I was a distance runner, and wasn't used to the feeling of spikes that were typically only used by sprinters. But without spikes, it would be impossible to run in the snow. Our coaches lathered our faces with a thick coating of Vaseline to protect against the cold and wind; it was the only part of my body that was exposed. With my thin clothes, I was already cold from the draft that was coming through the door. I tried to move closer to the heat vents that were blasting above the door entrance, but I didn't want to allow myself to get too warm before having to venture outside.

"Okay girls, it's three minutes until race time; get ready for the opening of the doors. Once we open the doors, assemble as quickly as you can on the starting line; the gun will go off shortly thereafter." The head of the race screamed through his megaphone into the crowded gymnasium. There wasn't even a starting line to see with the snow; in place of it they had tied a rope around two trees.

Blast off. The smoke from the gun faded into the snow swells, and we were off. I had to shove my way through the crowds. With the heavy snow underneath, it was hard to move, and some of the girls were having an especially difficult time, making the whole process a disaster. I pushed my elbows out as far as I could, creating a several foot space around my body to avoid the crowds. I almost wished I had my safety pin from Hong Kong; I smiled, recalling the densely packed sidewalks from Causeway Bay City. Focus on the race and stop daydreaming I told myself; I had to concentrate on getting out in front. Pretty soon I was out in the lead with two of my teammates and five other girls from another team; the eight of us broke free from the masses, keeping our heads down to avoid the biting wind as best we could. On the first incline, one of the girls fell while trying to climb the hill. Two of the other girls weren't able to move in time, and both of them trampled over the fallen down girl with their long spikes. I could see the red liquid ooze into the snow from her cuts. I felt guilty as we continued our race, but knew she would get help. I could feel by body numbing, but wouldn't give in to the pain; I was now in the top five, and wasn't going to succumb to anything.

I fell several times on the big hill, but all the runners were pretty spread out at this point, and I was able to get myself up without any injuries. I wondered what my time would be; I felt like I was barely running, but I wouldn't let myself stop to walk. I could see the finish line approaching, and surrounding the area was a mass of ambulances. I crossed the finish line in third place with a time of twenty-five minutes and four seconds. It was the slowest 5K I would ever run in my life. But it didn't matter; I had finished third in the state championships. Our team had captured the number one, two, three, and four slots. Even though I was again third for our team, I felt better not being number one; I was top in the state, and I had given everything I had to the race. My extra training had paid off, and there was no way I could have physically done any better than I did.

It had been a slow process, but I finally realized I wasn't capable of being number one on our team, no matter how much extra training I did. Our top runner, Cheri, had already qualified for the Olympics, and was being recruited by all the top college running programs. She barely tried when she ran; her natural abilities gave her an incredible head start against all of us. At everything in life, I would always be the person who worked twice as hard as everyone else. I would beat everyone when it came to passion and true obsession with anything I took on. No one on our team worked harder than I did, but even with that, the best I could do was number three. I would have to get used to not always being the best, something that wasn't necessarily easy for me. But beyond hard work, determination, and the energy I received from visualizing success, there was nothing else I could do.

I huddled with my teammates, slowly making our way into the gymnasium. We all looked like mountaineers coming in from a trek up Mount Everest. Our Vaseline coated faces were a blended shade of deep red and purple. I could barely open my eyes; the ice and snow that had built up on my eyelashes made it almost impossible to see. Our uniforms were covered in snow, dirt, and blood. The gymnasium was a chaotic sea of athletes crying, frantic coaches and parents looking for lost runners, and medical crews with stations set up throughout the facility. I scanned the room, trying to find our coaches and the several parents who had traveled with us. I couldn't feel my feet and was now having difficulty walking. I wanted to cry, but knew I had to hold it in and be strong. I wasn't sure if I wanted to cry because of my own pain, or because of everything I was looking at. I could see several athletes that appeared to be seriously injured, most of whom were being lifted onto stretchers to be taken away in ambulances. One girl I recognized from another team was unconscious, and a team of medics was doing CPR. I looked away, feeling both horrible for her, and relief that I wasn't the one lying on the floor.

We finally found our crew, and I collapsed onto the ground in pain, finally starting to cry at the relief of finding them. My coaches were screaming at us, "Congratulations girls, we're proud of you guys. It was tough out there, and you did it." They were consumed with us being tough; no matter what pain you ever felt, or what injury you ever had, unless it was a broken leg, there was no excuse for taking a break from running. Art Kranick, the male coach, had a set of tricks for temporarily healing any injury. He had studied acupressure, and would send many of us into tears, as he pressed his fingertips as hard as he could into our strained muscles. "Just suck it up; this will relieve the pressure." I was never sure if it did or not, but knew I had to tough it out regardless. I had bought every concoction for healing sore muscles – Ben Gay, Icy Hot, Green Dragon potion – I tried them all.

"It hurts, it hurts," I cried, arching my back, as Art took my shoes off for me. I was lying on the cold gymnasium floor, and my feet were in agony. I shuddered as he took off the first sock; my foot was purple, blue, and yellow. It looked like the foot of an alien to me. My other foot only looked and felt worse. One of the parents who had come with us held my ice cold feet against his bare stomach for the next hour, slowly easing the sensation back. I lay there, watching the blur of crying runners, medics, and ambulance crews, as I began to cry, unable to even say thanks to the poor father who was trying to help me.

I ended up being one of the lucky ones. I had fairly bad frostbite, but not bad enough to warrant a trip to the hospital. None of my teammates had sustained any serious injuries. The second ranked team in the state had only worn tank tops in the race, obsessed with the typical benefits of lightweight clothing when racing. The entire team was carried away by ambulance; every single one of them had hypothermia. The frostbite would last my lifetime, as the nerves never repaired themselves, but my third place finish would also last a lifetime. It was my best running race ever.

# Chapter 14 – Struggling to balance it all

Kyle and Ashley were excited that Linda would be with us another day. Although they clearly enjoyed the activities I would plan every Friday, they continued to ask about Linda when she wasn't around.

"Can Linda come with us to the zoo?" Kyle looked up at me, his large brown eyes always full of emotion. "I miss Linda," he added.

"Linda loo!" Ashley began chanting. "Linda loo. We want Linda loo!"

"Hey guys, Linda has the day off today. It's just mommy, Kyle, and Ashley. We're going to have fun!" I was trying to win over my kids; it seemed crazy. I was jealous of Linda, and I could almost sense the kids realizing it. I wanted to say something to make them not worship Linda so much, but I knew that was ridiculous. I was thankful for Linda's love towards our kids, but I was growing increasingly tired of feeling inferior around her. At the zoo, I pointed at everything around us, describing the different animals and sights. It was the way Linda did it, using every minute as a teaching moment. But it also reminded me of what my dad had done for me as a child. He had taken every moment to teach me things and challenge me to learn. I thought back to the many hours rock skipping, and all the silly little things my dad would point out.

Even though I was able to finish my Friday workload in four to five hours, Linda wouldn't allow me to interact with the kids until I was ready to send her home. She couldn't deal with the disruption this caused to the kids; their behavior was noticeably different around me, and it messed up their structured day. I was left to rush to complete what I could in the morning, and would send Linda home after half a day, even though I was stuck paying her for a whole day. Invariably, something at work would come up later in the day, and I'd be stuck without help. But I refused to continue hiding in my own house, hearing the kids, "Is Mommy home?" and Linda telling them no.

———ᴧᴧ———

"Kyle, quit taking Ashley's toys!" I screamed in exasperation into the large expanse of our over sized minivan while driving home from the day's morning activity. Brooks and I were again expecting another child. We had purchased the minivan to celebrate passing five months in the pregnancy, and learning that we would indeed have a healthy baby this time. The decision to purchase the minivan had been a tough decision that ultimately helped to destroy my image as a successful career woman. It led to incessant jibes from my college friends; even the valet attendants didn't hesitate to offer their commentary. "Oh yes, the kid mobile, we'll have that in a minute for you Ma'am." But in the end, the sheer convenience it offered – automatic doors and trunk, seventeen cup holders, low proximity to the ground – made it an almost necessity with kids. It allowed a frenzied Mom to avert disaster after potential disaster in a busy parking lot; simply being able to load both kids in at once avoided the likelihood of one darting off while I loaded the other. It was now a necessity with a third on the way.

Kyle was attempting to rip the arm off of Ashley's "Grover;"

Grover lay straddled in the space between their two car seats, one of his arms held by Ashley, and the other by Kyle.

"My Grover! My Grover!" Ashley screamed futility.

"I want it! I want it!" Kyle was taunting his sister to gain attention, an attempt to fill his boredom while driving.

"I see a fire truck," Kyle momentarily switched his attention, hearing the siren whiz by. "It's on my side," he proudly proclaimed.

"No it's not, it's on my side!" Ashley countered. They bantered back and forth, still both tugging on Grover.

Arguing over which side a particular car, truck, or building was on was for some reason an endless and futile battle. The twins were obsessed with wanting anything of interest to be on their side.

"Kids, enough already! It's on both of your sides, okay!"

My cell phone rang. I prided myself on being always reachable. I was constantly worried that something might happen to the kids, and maintained a personal rule that I would answer my cell phone almost no matter where I was. Sure enough, it was a 563 number, the digits for Freedom's internal system.

"Kyle and Ashley, please be quiet, I have to answer my phone," I pleaded in desperation. To date, work was under the impression I was sitting at a desk at home every Friday; I'd kept up the disguise so far, and couldn't blow it now. I had only been in my new position now for two months – an analyst and fund manager covering the investment banks. The phone rang for the third time. I quickly pulled over at a car wash, opened the door and ran around to the twins' side. I grabbed Grover from Kyle, threw it at Ashley, and then shut the door before I could hear the new round of fighting and crying that I had just started.

"It's Yolanda," I answered half out of breath at this point.

"Hey, it's Chuck, I wanted to tell you that it's just coming across the tape that Merrill is making an acquisition."

Great, I thought.   I didn't care whether it was good news for the stock or not.  I had a buy rating on Merrill, and I needed good news to drive the stock higher, which ultimately impacted my bonus.  But all I could think of now was how I was going to do the necessary work to follow up on the news and make it appear I was busy working from home.  This involved, first, the impossible at the moment, access to a computer.  Second, I needed to call the company.

"Thanks so much for calling to alert me, I'll get on it right away."

Chuck knew I wasn't always in front of my computer, and thought he was doing me a favor by calling on my cell.

I quickly flagged an attendant at the car wash.

I could hear Kyle and Ashley's arguing from behind the closed windows, still bantering back and forth, and now screaming, "Mommy, get back in the car!"

"Hey, do you have a chance to wash our car right now?"  I screamed over the rush of the washers.

"Sure, what service you want?  We have mini, the works, and the deluxe program.  The deluxe program includes…"

I could barely understand his response, between the clanking sounds the car wash created, the screams emanating from my minivan, and his broken English.

"Whatever, you pick, I don't have much time."

My goal was to distract the kids with the excitement of watching our car washed by a variety of exotic looking machines. What two year old wouldn't be mesmerized, at least for several minutes, by such a sight?   All I needed was ten minutes to make several phone calls.

"Okay, whatever lady, just move your car over by the red pole."

I jumped back in, backed the car up by the red pole, all the while looking up the phone number for my contact at Merrill.

"Hey guys, guess what, these men are going to wash our car. Want to get out and watch."

"Car wash? Yeah!" They screamed in unison.

I dragged them out of the car as quickly as possible, and planted them on the grass next to the car wash area.

"Now be quiet, the men washing the car don't like us to make any noise. If we make noise they'll come yell at us."

The fear of reprimand by a third party was always useful in any order I needed them to listen to. Kyle looked up at me with fear in his eyes, settling quietly onto the grass and fixating in on the whiz of brushes now working on our minivan.

I dialed my contact at Merrill.

"Hey Craig, it's Yolanda from Freedom. I don't have a lot of time, can you give me the scoop on the acquisition?"

The secretary had been trained to always put through the Freedom call; I was fortunate that Craig was currently available. I jotted down what he said on the back of an animal cracker box, the only thing other than a diaper I had to write on, trying to mouth silently to Kyle and Ashley as Craig spoke. As I was asking Craig to repeat what he had just said and accurately record it on the animal box, Kyle and Ashley discovered the puddles from the car wash next to where we were sitting.

"Puddles!" The twins began to scream in delight.

I reached out to grab one of their hands, but it was too late. Both kids were dripping with mud, their squeals of delight drowned against the many background noises.  It wasn't worth attempting to put Craig on hold to minimize the damage. I was still listening to him go on about how accretive and strategically positive the acquisition was. I copied down his words, my weak attempt to impress work with my diligence and timeliness at the breaking of any relevant news.

"Great, I think I've gotten all I need," I cut him off after three minutes.

"Are you sure?  Don't you have any questions? Well, I'm around all day if you decide you have follow up questions."

I hung up and turned to look at the mess my twins had made. They had mud all over their faces. Innocent eyes looked up at me, the only part of their face that was visible behind the brown sludge. The puddles were deep and filled with suds from the car wash. The soapy bubbles along with the mud covered their bodies.

"Ugh," I sighed to myself. "Guys, you are a mess! Let's strip down."

It was only about fifty degrees, not exactly appropriate weather to be out with naked children, but they were soaked, and I didn't have any spare clothes with me. I stripped them both, wringing out their clothes on the ground. As an after thought, I decided it was easiest to toss the clothes in the trash. The twins had closets full of stuff – one T-shirt and a pair of pants would surely not be missed.

"Excuse me sir?" I screamed as loud as I could to get the attention of the car wash attendant. "Is our car almost done? We really need to get out of here."

"Probably another ten or fifteen minutes Mam."

Great, the kids are going to freeze, I still had to leave a voicemail at work on my thoughts on the acquisition, and we were stuck outside in the cold.

"Do you have two towels I can borrow?"

The man smiled, or perhaps smirked, as he noticed my now naked children, and brought two grease stained towels over to me. I draped them over Kyle and Ashley and then pulled the bribe trick to try to get them to keep quiet for a minute.

"Hey guys, if you stay quiet while Mommy is on the phone I'll buy you ice-cream on the way home."

"Ice-cream, Ice-cream! I want a big one," Kyle screamed.

"I want two ice-creams," Ashley responded.

Naked wet kids and ice cream, what a great combination I thought. I'd be sure to win "Mom of the year" award for this adventure.

"Okay, okay," Just be quiet for a minute. I quickly dialed

into my work voicemail, left the message as quickly as I could, and then breathed a sigh of relief. I had made it look like I was all over the acquisition, that I was working from home as expected on a Friday. Safe again I thought to myself. We drove home, got ice cream from the take out at McDonalds, and everyone was happy. Just in time for naptime.

———∧∧——

The kids were sound asleep, and I was enjoying my two hours of freedom. It was my time to get in any semblance of a workout. I was obsessed with my daily workouts; if I didn't get to workout on a daily basis, I couldn't sleep at night.    I had taken the necessary fifteen minutes to write up my note from the Merrill news of the morning, and was just changed and heading into our basement workout room. My cell phone rang again. A 563 number, ugh.

"Hi, it's Yolanda." I answered in my serious work voice, assuming it was a quick follow up question on the Merrill deal.

"Oh hey Yolanda, it's Chuck again, I was wondering if you could look into something...."

He was calling again with another seemingly important work item. They were always important, that was the nature of the stock market. Most of what we did, researching companies, was optional. There wasn't a clear correlation between good analysis and high knowledge level of a company's inner workings and actually picking the stock correctly. But if you didn't treat every facet of a company's business seriously, you were at risk for ignoring the infrequent and irregular major news item that sent the stock on a wild up or down ride. I couldn't afford to ignore Chuck's suggestion.

"Sure, I'll get right on it," I responded as eagerly as I could muster.

It should be fine; the kids are asleep, probably still an hour before wake up time. It would kill my workout plans, but the temperature had now warmed up to the sixties. I would bribe the twins into a trip to town in the jogging stroller. I quickly got to work. This could be a two-hour project, but I was determined to get it done in thirty minutes. The kids were very sensitive to any noise during naptime. I grabbed my laptop, the phone, and a notepad and rushed outside to make a phone call. After getting the necessary data on the phone, I quietly moved back inside to type up my conclusions and send an email to work. Send. Another potential crisis averted. Just then the house phone rang, one of the calls I had made returning my call. I grabbed the phone and my laptop and rushed outside again to take the call, hoping the sound of the ring wouldn't wake the kids. Of course it had; I heard the first cry as I shut the door behind me. I tripped on the step, my laptop went into the air as I tried to catch myself and not hurt the growing baby in my belly.

"Hi, it's Yolanda," I took a deep breath and tried not to sound flustered.

The laptop was in pieces. I brushed away my mounting stress. I had sent the email I needed to; work again assumed everything was calm and under control on my work from home Friday. I would conjure up a story of how my laptop broke while on a business trip; Freedom's deep pockets allowed such carelessness to go unnoticed.

I was exhausted, now five months pregnant, and working as hard as I had my first several years at Freedom. But I thrived on the challenge of trying to do it all, and I knew I would get a break in another four months. I was already looking forward to maternity leave, and the extra time I would get home with Kyle and Ashley.

~᳁~

"Damn it!" I yelled. I couldn't help myself.

I was at the airport with our summer intern, and they had cancelled our flight. We were on our way home from meetings in Newark, NJ. I wasn't even supposed to be on the business trip anyway, but thought I'd be a good mentor and accompany the summer intern. I had meetings in New York City in the morning. Manish, the intern, had asked if I'd join him in Newark in the afternoon. It was a simple addition to my trip, and his meeting was scheduled to end by three p.m.; I assumed the incremental effort would be worth it. I'd be on the four p.m. flight home, still in time to have a normal evening with the kids. I was Manish's mentor, and as his mentor was supposed to help him with every aspect of his summer assignment. I felt incessant guilt for every moment I didn't devote to Manish's development. Manish had already fallen behind his peers in his knowledge and conviction of the companies he covered; I felt personally responsible for his success, and knew I had to do whatever I could to help him in his analysis. I already sensed that the situation was futile; he just didn't have a sense of how the markets worked. But I couldn't give up without giving it my best effort.

"Yes, I'm with Freedom. Our Continental flight back to Boston was just cancelled, are there any other available flights?" I quickly got on the phone to our travel department.

Manish stood there dumfounded, lacking experience in how to react quickly to travel situations.

"Great, book me on that. Yes, I think we can make it." "Go Manish, run, there's a flight on US Air in fifteen minutes. It's in Terminal A, but if we run, I think we can make it." We were off. I was six months pregnant, dashing through the airport like a fool. Manish insisted on carrying my heavy duffel bag; my pocketbook and laptop bag bounded against my large belly as I ran in heels. I insisted on wearing heels throughout the pregnancy. At five feet tall, I needed all the help I could get to make me appear more credible as a businesswoman. We arrived at the US Air terminal with three minutes to spare. The waiting area was filled with travelers who were clearly disgruntled.

"Ugh, you've got to be kidding me!" I screamed. I looked up at the monitor, seeing the words cancelled or delayed run down the entire right side of the display. Our US Air flight was not going anywhere.

I redialed out travel department, "Yes, yes, I'm with Freedom. Listen, you booked us on US Air, and that's now cancelled, what are our options?" I screamed in exasperation at the helpless attendant on the line.

"Let's hustle," I yelled to Manish, "It looks like our original flight is now going. If we run, we can make it back to Terminal B."

Again, we took off at full stride. The terminals were at least a half-mile apart. A half-mile cluttered with food vendors, gadget vendors, and slow walking travelers with wheelie bags. We darted in and out of the hazards, moving as fast as we possibly could.

I stumbled on the ramp, not seeing that the floor had started to incline. I landed smack on my belly. My eyes began to well up, but I quickly held back the tears, not wanting Manish to see. Manish was an eager twenty two year old; he was single and didn't have children. How could he relate to everything that was rushing through my mind? I've killed my baby. I was sure of it. I glanced down to see if there was any blood. A crowd had formed around me.

"Are you okay?" A nice man bent down to grab my hand and pull me up.

"I think so." "No, nothing hurts." I tried to remain calm, but all I wanted to do was sit down and bawl. And I wanted my doctor.

"Don't worry, my wife did the same thing when she was pregnant, and everything was completely fine," The man tried to comfort me.

It did give me some comfort, but I had my hand on my belly, and I couldn't feel any kicking. I feared the worst.

We sat in the Newark terminal for hours until we were able to get on another flight back to Boston. My well thought out plan to be home in time for dinner with the kids was now a distant memory. I called the doctor and three different friends to get some reassurance.

"Drink some orange juice and then sit still. You should feel the baby kicking shortly thereafter. If it does, everything is probably okay." The doctors tried to reassure me everything would be fine.

I bought my orange juice and sat down in the closest available seat. Nothing. Another sip. Nothing. I finished the entire bottle. All of a sudden I thought I felt something. Or did I just burp? Was that just a cramp? Now I didn't know what to do. Was it a kick? I couldn't be sure. I almost bought another bottle of juice, but then it was time to board the plane, and it was all I could do to make the flight back home before breaking down in tears.

The doctors told me weeks later that there was blood in my placenta, but they didn't want to alarm me. Instead, they reassured me that everything was okay during my appointment the following day. At the subsequent appointment they explained that the blood was gone, and my pregnancy was progressing well. My fall helped to slow me down for about a week. But then I was back, running for flights, trying to prove to everyone that I could manage it all, pregnant, with two-year-old twins at home.

———∿∿———

We were at the Watertown fair with Linda. It was a beautiful Saturday afternoon in September. Kyle and Ashley took their first pony rides. I sat on the side, snapping picture after picture as Linda held Kyle on the horse, and Brooks held Ashley. I rubbed my belly, day dreaming of the baby we would soon have; I wondered if it was a boy or a girl. I was due in three weeks, and most of the preparations were now complete.

Kyle was laughing as Linda tickled him while helping him off the pony. "Smile," I yelled, snapping a picture of the two of them. I felt a pang of envy as Kyle held onto Linda.

"Look Kyle, that's a rose, let's smell it." She smiled as she helped Kyle bend down and smell the roses. "Do you know what these sharp things are on the stem of the rose?" Linda went on to explain to Kyle everything about roses, how there were many different colors, and how roses were a symbol of love. I never thought to explain to a kid something that seemed so above their intellect; but Kyle was fascinated, and responded with appropriate questions. I watched everything that Linda did, learning from her, and imitating her style of teaching. I was both proud and jealous when Kyle and Ashley started singing the alphabet song. Proud that they knew the alphabet at only age two, but jealous and embarrassed that it was Linda who had taught them the alphabet. I was ashamed that I hadn't even thought to try.

"Hey guys, should we go paint a pumpkin?" I pointed to a booth where the kids could paint their own pumpkins.

"I want to paint so many pumpkins!" Kyle screamed. Kyle always wanted two of everything, or "so many" of anything you offered him. Kyle had several favorite words – now, no, and so many. He was spoiled and I knew it; I also knew it was my fault. I rationalized that he was only two, and there was plenty of time to teach him the value of money. I still vowed to make him work as soon as he was able; I vowed to give the twins chores and teach them to save what they earned. Paper routes were no longer available for young kids, but they could baby sit and help around the house. I had years before any of this was relevant, and I could easily undo the overindulgences now. My dad had surprisingly never commented on our remodeled basement that was now overflowing with toys. He never drew comparisons between how I was raised and how I was raising my kids. I had caught him once noticing the Raggedy Ann doll I had purchased the twins while pregnant; the one that was now buried under a pile of other stuff animals – penguins, giraffes, dinosaurs, and other creatures the twins preferred. I had wondered if he was thinking what I was, remembering the Raggedy Ann doll he had given me as a kid, my only real toy.

I rubbed my belly again as we helped Kyle and Ashley glue colored cotton balls onto their pumpkins.

"Are you okay?" Linda asked, watching me.

"Yeah, I think so," I whispered to her. "I keep getting these cramps, and I was up all night last night with a weird feeling." I never thought much of sleepless nights. I was a horrible sleeper. My insomnia, which had developed while together with Mike, had surprisingly come back after a brief respite. The first several months sleeping with Brooks were wonderfully restful; I bounded out of bed each morning after eight peaceful hours of sleep. It was the first sign that Brooks was the right one. But it wasn't long before I found my mind occupied with work, the kids, and everything I needed to do. Sleep to me was a time to make lists. I would lie awake most nights making lists of things I had to do. Take ground beef out to make lasagna. Take clothes out of dryer. Buy gift for Tom's party. I had my little black book I carried with me everywhere. It was filled with list after list. I took comfort each day in being able to check items off the list. When there wasn't much on the list, I'd find myself making up to do's. I'd decide the picture in the blue bedroom wasn't just right, and make a note to find a new picture. I was obsessed with productivity and completing tasks. Sleep, or not sleeping, had unfortunately become another obsession of mine. As much as I wanted to break the cycle of insomnia, I couldn't; the experience with Mike had taken away my ability to shut down my brain and relax in bed.

"Maybe the baby's coming." Linda laughed, lighting up with excitement.

"Yeah, right, you know I'm not ready." I replied.

Linda knew how dependent I was on her. Having a third child would only make me rely on her more. The one day a week when Linda didn't work had become increasingly chaotic; the twins refused to nap on Fridays, and their behavior suffered as a result. Weekends were similar, and come Monday morning, Kyle and Ashley were exhausted and irritable. But Linda could put them in order instantly, with only a slight look of her eye. She'd smile as I stood by watching her, clearly helpless in my own home. Linda would invariably comment every Monday night when I returned home, "Today was a little off; it always takes most of Monday to get them back into listening after their weekends with you."

"Mommy, I'm done." Ashley was holding up her pumpkin.

"Beautiful, I love it. What is it?"

"It's a penguin!" She replied. Ashley was obsessed with penguins. "Penguin! Penguin!" She loved to scream out the word in public. I winced as the workers in the booth started laughing at her commentary.

"What's wrong babe?" Brooks now noticed I wasn't feeling very well.

"I don't know, maybe I should call the doctor." I called the easy to remember phone number – 724-BABY.

The nurse asked me all the labor questions. "Where does it hurt? How bad is the pain? Can you breathe?" She decided I wasn't in labor, that I was probably just having false contractions, and to go home, take a walk, and relax.

"So, what do you want to do?" Brooks was at the car, loading the twins in to return home.

"I'm fine, they said I'm not in labor. Let's go home and have lunch." I was looking forward to my daily work out during the twins' nap.

"Please call if anything changes, I will be waiting by my phone." Linda looked crestfallen. Linda couldn't wait for the new baby. She couldn't wait to cuddle it and rock it to sleep. She couldn't wait to teach it to sit up, to babble, and to crawl. I was excited to have the pregnancy over. I was excited to have three children and feel that sense of completeness in our family. I wasn't looking forward to all the extra work that would come with a third child. And the baby stage, the baby stage was so difficult. We had already signed up to have a baby nurse. We also had a baby nurse for the twins, but only for six weeks. This time we had committed to three months. It seemed a luxury, but we could afford it, and I justified it to myself. We were both working, and I was planning to work during maternity leave; Kyle and Ashley needed our full attention.

I had assumed having a third child on the way would give me the final push I needed to quit work, but without even thinking, I had voluntarily agreed to almost no maternity leave. I had just taken on a new assignment, and as they told me, had to reprove myself. It wasn't realistic to take a real maternity leave. I rationalized my decision both for work and personal reasons. It got me off the hook from breast-feeding. Carole regularly pitched the benefits of breast-feeding to me.

"Did you read the article I sent you?" She had sent another pro breast-feeding article. It was probably the third during the pregnancy. This one was particularly biased, claiming bottle fed babies faced severe health risks over time.

"Yeah, I did, thanks." I tried to quickly change the subject. "Kyle really likes that puzzle you gave him for his birthday." Was the point of the article to make me feel guilty for what had already been done with Kyle and Ashley, or to convince me that I could correct my mistakes with the third kid?

"What did you think?"

"Oh, about the article? It was interesting. You know, I'm pretty committed to my plan. It will be difficult to breast-feed once I'm back at work, and work expects me back within six weeks." My plan was to only pump for six weeks, and not really ever breast-feed at all. It was what I had done with the twins, and I felt obligated to do the same with the third kid. Pumping helped the uterus contract back to its normal size during the first six weeks; after that, the benefits were minimal.

～ΛΛ～

"Stop the car!" I screamed. We were on our way to the hospital. On the way home from the fair, my cramps worsened. I decided the nurses were wrong, and I was in labor no matter what they said. We called Linda as soon as we got home, and she rushed over to take care of Kyle and Ashley. I opened the car door and threw up on the side of the road.

"Okay babe, we're almost there, how far apart are the contractions now?" Brooks, as usual, was the calm one. We had been through this before, but it was different with the twins. I was on labor watch for weeks, expecting to deliver prematurely. With a single baby, I had assumed I'd go full-term. With the twins, my water broke, but I only experienced a few contractions. This time, there was no water, but an excruciating amount of pain.

Brooks left me in front of Massachusetts General Hospital while he quickly pulled around to park. I could barely stand, leaning against the cold stone wall to catch my breath while I waited for him.

"It's a Kaden!" Brooks screamed in delight as I did my final push. Out came a boy. We had debated names for the past four months. If it was a boy it was going to start with a K, like Kyle. If it was a girl, it was going to start with an A, like Ashley. I didn't cry this time, as I had with the twins, but sighed in delight as I heard the cries of health.

"Six pounds, four ounces," the nurse announced as she pulled Kaden off the scale. I was thrilled. I was very petite, Brooks was thin, Kyle and Ashley were both less than six pounds, and Kaden was several weeks early. I was proud to deliver a healthy baby. The last nine months passed over my memory in a blur.

In the labor room I had been frantically emailing work. I was scheduled to host two meetings the following week. I had completed all the prep just advance, and was able to email my boss from my hand held computer. I needed to make sure work knew I was on the ball, even in labor. Minutes after Kaden was born I sent an email to work, agreeing to host a meeting in six days time. I figured my belly would have shrunk enough by then, and it was an easy way to justify my night nurse. No matter what the circumstance, I had to win; I wanted to be the best at delivering a baby and resuming work quickly.

# Chapter 15 – The value of a life

I was surprised at how easily I transitioned back to work after Kaden was born. I now had three kids at home, and had barely recovered from the brief maternity leave. But I became reenergized about the business, quickly returning to traveling, and enjoying the challenges of investment work. However, my guilt about not being home only escalated. Kyle and Ashley were at a peak learning age, soaking up everything they heard, and starting to ask meaningful questions. The impact Linda was having on them was increasing by the day.

Brooks was noticeably proud that I worked at Freedom. When we got engaged, I remember him saying, "Wow, this is a bonus; I always assumed my wife wouldn't make any money." I tucked the comment away, trying not to read too much into it.

We were at the dinner table, having our almost daily conversation.

"Honestly, I just want you to be happy; there's nothing else I can say."

"But your mom stayed home. Even all your good friends say you're that type of guy. The guy who always visualized the house with the white picket fence and the wife at home baking pies."

"That might be true, but I fell in love with you."

I didn't know what to make of his comments. Did he fall in love with me despite his long held dreams? Was I a disappointment? I constantly struggled with who I wanted to be. I was surprised at how much I had changed since meeting Brooks. I could previously never imagine staying home to be just a mom, nor could I imagine preparing dinner for my husband each day. But after falling in love with Brooks, the most important thing became family. I wanted to have both a successful career and be an amazing mom, but I wasn't sure it was possible to be exceptional at both. Was I ready to give up the competitive drive that for so long had defined who I was? Was it possible to be just a mom and hold on to it?

I'd hear Brooks at parties. "My wife works at Freedom. She's one of the top women there." He seemed so proud.

———⌒∧∧⌒———

We hired a second nanny to help Linda several hours of the day. We now had three kids under the age of three, and I didn't want the demands of an infant to take away from Kyle and Ashley's enrichment. My work guilt only escalated with the addition of the extra help; although I was doing it solely for the kids, I was embarrassed to tell friends we had two nannies. I had always been embarrassed as a kid that we had so little; now I was embarrassed that we had so much.

Linda quickly decided she did not like Hale. Linda's primary fault was her stubbornness and rigidity. She was only content if she was in charge, and could not tolerate any deviation from her routine. Hale created a factor of uncertainty, and was something that Linda could not control. It took only several days with Linda and Hale working together before Linda was calling and emailing me, doing everything she could to make Hale look bad. "Hale can't feed Kaden," she would say. "Hale almost let Kaden fall off the changing table today." I had yet to witness any of Linda's accusations. Hale was Brazilian and a fantastic cook; her first day on the job she made the twins a fluffy omelet reminiscent of the ones my dad had made me as a kid. For dinner she made them lentil soup. The twins had never eaten so well, and my frustrations with Linda's gravitation towards junk food had only increased.

"I can't work with her." Linda was matter of fact and blunt in her delivery. Hale had been with us less than two weeks. "I don't need the help anyway; Kaden is easy, it's not a big deal to have all three on my own."

"But what will you do when Kaden has to nap? You'll be stuck at home more often." I tried to convince her she needed the help. Linda hated spending the day at home, but was also a stickler for schedules, and Kaden napped four to five hours of each day.

"Well, we'll just have to stay home more often while he's on his current nap schedule." She was quick with a comeback. "I already bought several workbooks to work on the alphabet." I had recently given Linda a credit card to use for family purchases, and her love of spending was quickly showing through. Not a day went by where she didn't buy something new to help stimulate the kids' development. I couldn't say anything, because everything she purchased was indeed very creative and stimulating. But I worried that she was becoming addicted to the credit line. As much as I wanted to take the credit card away, realizing the conveniences it offered weren't enough to offset the increasing dependence it created in our relationship, I couldn't. Linda would be too insulted, a risk I wasn't willing to take. What could I say to defend Hale when Linda could clearly manage on her own, and was offering to work more on our children's development?

Firing Hale was a disaster. She said what I knew was true, but there was nothing I could do to defend myself.

"You let Linda run your house. It's ridiculous. Why does she get to decide whether I can work here or not?"

"Well, Hale, Linda has been here a long time, and it's important that she be happy." My retort was weak but true.

"But why isn't she happy? I make her lunch, I clean up for her. How could she not like that?" Hale was now crying. "I changed my schedule so that I could work the hours you wanted me to. Now you've messed up my whole life." Hale was a student, and had modified her entire class schedule so that she could fit school into our requirements. She was right, and I felt terrible.

I was dependent on Linda to keep my job, and to keep stability in our lives. If Linda left, it would be too disruptive to my work and the children. The kids loved her, and knew Linda as a member of our family.

I wondered if I could work with Linda if I stayed home. I wasn't sure I would be able to stay home and have no help, yet at the same time, if I were to stay home, it would be my job. I would be embarrassed to no longer make any money, but spend money to have someone help me take care of my kids. I had never had any help on my days home, and as much as I loved it that way, there was almost no free time. I wasn't sure I'd be able to get my daily workouts in, and I surely would not be able to do anything other than take care of the kids all day. I didn't think my identity could handle giving up working entirely, and not retaining something that would be just for myself. I wasn't sure what it would be, but I knew I would have to find something, even if it was pure volunteer work. I had become involved in the town PTA after the twins were born, and I envisioned spending more time on some of that work. I knew moms who stayed home, had full time help, and spent half their day at the gym and the spa. I knew I could never be like that and retain my sense of self-respect, but at the same time, I knew I couldn't be one of those moms who had no help and no outside interests or involvement other than spending time with their kids. I wasn't sure there could be a balance that would make me happy if I stayed home.

My dad had surprised me with his subtle comments after Kyle and Ashley were born. "You must really miss the munchkins during the day," he would casually say. "There's nothing more rewarding than raising a kid and being there for them every minute of the day." Perhaps his benign comments carried no meaning, but I insisted on reading into them. Carl, the father who had pushed me every step of the way, seemed to want me home taking care of my kids.

Carl insisted I was never sick as a kid, and was surprised at the incessant ear infections and fevers that seemed to plague our house. "You were only sick once that I can distinctly remember," he recalled, reminding me of when my fever spiked above one hundred and five as a four year old. My dad had spent a week by my side, checking my temperature every two hours, and holding my hand in the bathtub he continually filled with ice cubes. His only job was taking care of me and making sure I got better; he wasn't conflicted with having to miss work meetings to stay home with a sick kid.

I returned home each evening to overflowing laundry and dishes; every room in the house was strewn with toys. I spent at least two hours each night after work folding laundry and cleaning up. I wanted to ask Linda to clean up after the kids, but I couldn't. I was scared it would make her angry. She seemed to view housework as being beneath her position. I was dependent on Linda, and she knew it. I found myself always going out of my way to keep her happy. It started with small additions to her pay; a pattern that led to a salary increase of more than thirty percent in two years. I occasionally gave her small gifts – treats that were soon expected. The first time she called in sick, I went out of my way to tell her it was perfectly fine; it wasn't long before she was calling in sick every time she had a moderate cough. She missed six weeks of work in her first year with us. I never said anything about it. She left early every time there was a small amount of snow on the roads. She was paid until seven p.m. each night, but never worked past six p.m. She had grown used to it, and although she knew she was still being paid, would rush out the door as soon as I got home at 6.

I was so focused on returning home by six p.m. each night that I soon forgot Linda was technically obligated to stay until seven. I had recently left numerous meetings at work early, meetings that were supposed to end at five, but would often drag on, running thirty minutes late. I would look at my watch over and over as the time approached five, fidgeting in my seat as I stressed about what to do. Should I stay until the end? If it only runs another ten minutes, I can still be in my car by five-thirty, and home by six fifteen. But if it runs over another thirty minutes, then I might as well just leave now and deal with the consequences of incessantly leaving early. I still cared about what people thought at work, and knew of the damage I was doing by always being the first to walk out, but I refused to stay later. Brooks always arrived home between six thirty and seven; I wanted to be the first to return home and see the kids. I loved the smiles that would light up on their faces when they saw me walk in the door; they would run to me, all three of them jumping into my arms. Brooks didn't get this same reaction as the second one to arrive home. I wasn't willing to give that up, even though I knew it was damaging my reputation at work.

———∿∧∽———

"Kyle, quit pulling stuff off the shelves!" We had all three kids at the grocery store. Even though the night nurse was still living with us and watching Kaden, we felt guilty not taking him during the day. But trying to run errands with three kids was a comedy of adventures.

"Spider Man!" Kyle screamed as he pointed at the Spiderman cheese crackers. "I want those!"

"Here, fine, take them," I sighed in frustration, handing him another snack pack. I tried to strategically avoid the aisles with the themed snacks, but it was impossible. All you had to do was put Spiderman, Dora, or Sponge Bob on top of a box of crackers, and the kids thought they were the best crackers in the world.

"I want Dora crackers." Now it was Ashley's turn to start. It was impossible to get out of the grocery store without buying each of them a pile of new snacks. I rationalized that it was food; it wasn't like taking them to the toy store and letting them pick out every toy they wanted. I thought back to my days growing up. I didn't even know what snacks were. You ate three meals a day – breakfast, lunch, and dinner; you ate whatever was put on the table. Before having kids I swore that my kids wouldn't be picky eaters. They would also eat whatever I put on the table. But our kids were skinny. Kyle was so skinny that he wasn't even on the weight charts. It was clearly genetic, but either way, it made me obsessive about their meals. I was determined to make sure they ate a lot. "I don't want that!" was almost always screamed during a meal. It could have been something they loved just the day before. "I don't like meatballs!" Ashley proclaimed only hours after announcing that meatballs were her favorite food in the world. I gave them whatever they wanted to eat in desperation. "Just take three bites, and I'll give you a cookie." I would use any bargaining tactic I could think of. Getting through a meal often required me to heat up three separate dinners. I tried to tell myself that hungry kids would eventually eat, but I didn't have the patience to test the theory. The doctors were making us weigh Kyle every three months, and it was my responsibility to get his weight up in whatever way possible.

As we pulled into the garage, Kaden began screaming for his bottle. Kyle and Ashley were busy fighting over who had seen the red car on the street. "I saw it!" "No you didn't, I saw it!" It was the typical irrational conversation held between two 2 year olds; there was nothing you could say to reason with them. I unbuckled Kyle and Ashley, leaving them to get out of the car themselves, and rushed inside to prepare Kaden's bottle. Brooks began unloading the groceries, paying no attention to Kyle and Ashley as they continued fighting.

"Brooks, where's Ashley?" I was sitting with Kaden at the table, Brooks was cleaning up the kitchen, and I could hear Kyle playing with his trains. We'd been home fifteen minutes, and I hadn't noticed or heard from Ashley since.

"I don't know, maybe she went upstairs," he answered casually. Kyle and Ashley now more or less safely wandered the house by themselves, but it was never long before they got into trouble and required our attention. It was rare for one to go upstairs without the other. Brooks walked out of the kitchen, about to go upstairs, and suddenly started screaming.

"Ashley, Ashley!" He yelled as he rushed over to the corner to pick her up. Ashley was slumped in the corner by the door, visibly blue and not moving. Brooks picked her up, screaming in panic, "Ashley, Ashley, wake up!"

I grabbed the phone and dialed 911, surprising myself with my speed in getting 911 on the phone. I'd often imagined emergency situations, and feared that I'd panic and freeze. I didn't know what was happening, but I held the confidence that everything would be okay as long as we got an ambulance to our house as soon as possible. Brooks turned Ashley upside down, assuming she was choking on something and started banging her back.

"Ann, Ann!" He screamed. Ann was Kaden's night nurse who lived with us. She had decades of experience taking care of children.

I chimed in. "Ann, Ann!" I yelled as loud as I could. "Ann, come downstairs."

"She's choking." Ann instantly diagnosed the situation as soon as she saw Ashley. "Get her upside down and use the heel of your hand to bang in the middle of her back. Bang it very hard." Brooks started banging harder and harder, panicking at the lack of response.

"Yes, hello, my daughter seems to be choking. She can't breathe." I spoke to the operator at 911. I'd never called 911 before, and was surprised at the efficiency with which they answered the phone and proceeded to ask me questions.

"How old is she? How long has she been unconscious? Where do you live?" I calmly answered all of their questions, while watching Brooks' and Ann's so far futile attempts to revive Ashley.

Ashley finally regained consciousness, after what seemed to be many minutes. I held back my tears of relief, as I ran over to Brooks to take her in my arms. Ashley was now breathing, but could barely hold her head up. She lay her head down on my shoulder, her eyelids fluttering.

"Ash, are you okay?" Brooks was trying to get her to respond.

"Ash honey, are you okay?" I rubbed her cheeks, trying to get her to perk up.

Ann watched on with concern, holding Kaden who was oblivious to what was going on. Kyle was in the adjoining room, paying no attention. I only realized later how odd it was that he wasn't aware of Ashley's distress.

Ashley finally responded, whimpering, "I'm okay." I could barely hear her.

911 was still on the phone, continuing to ask me questions. "Hi, yes, she seems to be okay now. She must have been choking. You don't need to come anymore."

The ambulance insisted on coming anyway; they doubted that it was a choking incident when I told them that nothing came out of her mouth. The ER team consisted of two fire trucks and four police trucks. Neighbors came out to see what all the commotion was. They diagnosed a febrile seizure, a seizure brought on by a sudden fever. It was fairly common in children, and was almost always outgrown by age five. Ashley fell asleep on top of me on the way to the hospital. I still hadn't shed a tear. I knew staying calm was necessary, and I had to be strong for my daughter. Ashley was wearing her new white argyle sweater and jeans that day, an image that would forever stay in my mind. I would never forget what she looked like when she was blue and barely breathing.

I had become increasingly emotional since having kids, a trait that I still hadn't learned to deal with after years of my father forcing me to hide my emotions. My initial excuse was the fertility medicines that caused my hormones to get all out of whack. I had even started crying for no apparent reason during an IVF cycle while golfing with Brooks. But the fertility medicines were now long out of my system, and I still found myself breaking down at seemingly inconsequential things; things that I would have been embarrassed to even care about in the past. I was both proud and ashamed at how I was able to maintain my composure during Ashley's seizure. I knew I loved her unconditionally, but perhaps I was scared of letting everyone else see how much. Perhaps I was scared of losing too much of myself in my kids. I had assumed it was a given that they would be with us forever; but what if the time with them wasn't forever? These thoughts had never entered my mind on a daily basis. My days were too consumed with rushing off to work everyday, leaving Linda in charge of our house; there wasn't time to stop and think.

Linda had rushed to the hospital with her mother when I called to tell her what had happened. She made her mother accompany her because she was crying so much. She showed up at the hospital distraught and in tears. I felt guilty that Linda was crying and I still hadn't shed a tear. Linda was an emotional person in general, but her obvious and overt love for Kyle, Ashley, and Kaden consistently made me feel awkward. They were my kids, and yet to a stranger passing by on the street, one would think they belonged to Linda. If the five of us were out together, Kyle and Ashley would instantly grab onto Linda's hands instead of mine; fortunately, Kaden was still a baby, and enjoyed being held. Linda would think nothing of how this made me feel, and would bend down to kiss Kyle and Ashley, relishing the attention they showered on her.    I constantly rationalized that I had the nanny that anyone would dream of; the nanny that in every way treated my kids like her own.  I was able to leave for work every morning, knowing they were in great hands.  I felt that they were better off in her care than they would be in mine.  I was not as patient as Linda, I didn't have the experience Linda did, and I was not as structured and disciplined as Linda.  But they were my kids; something didn't feel right.

The weeks following Ashley's seizure I did cry.   Brooks and I both cried that night in bed when the chaos of the day had finally ended.  Ashley never recalled a second of the day. Surprisingly, Kyle, who had witnessed everything, also didn't recall anything.  They say there is something in the brain that triggers amnesia to block out painful events.  I, however, visualized the day over and over.  After all the pain we had gone through to have children, the thought of losing one of them was the worst thing I could ever imagine.

I added Ashley's seizure to my list of reasons for why I should quit work.  I always felt that I needed reasons. Wanting to be a mom and spend more time with my kids wasn't enough. After Kyle and Ashley were born, I approached work, asking to reduce my hours to part-time.  My reasons were Ashley's slow development and the fact that I was pregnant and about to have a third child fifteen months after having twins.  I was struggling with the adjustment to motherhood, and by assembling a list of reasons no one could challenge I was able to justify my waning interest in work.   Ashley had thrived after six months of early intervention, and she no longer needed my extra attention.  My pregnancy had ended in miscarriage.  Now my reasons were having three children under the age of three and the fear that we could lose one of our children at any moment.  Ashley's seizure made me realize that my fear of losing a child was legitimate. It also made me realize that I would do anything for my children.

I started writing my thoughts down on a piece of paper, with a column for pros of leaving work and a column for cons of leaving work. My pro column was filling up with the obvious items − three young kids, Ashley's seizure, increased home demands. But at the same time I added to the pro column, I continued to add to the con column − financial dependence on Brooks, loss of competitive streak, loss of identity, intellectual void. Every point in both columns was subjective and impossible to assign a value to; I couldn't add the points and pick a winner. Without a scientific answer to my dilemma, I didn't know what to do.

# Chapter 16 – Reflecting back

My dad was thrilled with my gift proposal.

"Wow kiddo, seriously? You're going to pay for both of us to go back to Redway? That would be terrific." He didn't explain why he had never considered going back before; it was obviously an expensive trip, but my dad was making enough money now that he could have afforded a trip back. He didn't realize that I was partially doing the trip for me. I wanted to see what it was really like. My memories had become increasingly foggy, and in making my work decision, I longed to see the environment my dad raised me in. I wanted to go alone with my dad, an opportunity for both of us to relive the old days, and appreciate how far we had come.

My dad contacted several of his friends to inform them of our pending visit. Friends contacted friends, and within several days, most of the town was in the midst of planning a party to welcome us back. We were viewed as the single father with the kid who had pudgy cheeks; even for those that didn't remember us well, their memories were brought to life with that mention. When we had left California, we were seen as heroes. Residents of Redway were thrilled to learn that we had survived, and not only had we made it alive, but that Carl had raised me to be a successful grown woman. I had been known in town for my obsession with money; everyone cheered to learn that I had indeed succeeded in my dreams.

My dad's friend Steve insisted on hosting us. Paco would host the party, and we would stay with Steve and his wife. I had distinct images of Paco, but did not remember Steve well. My friend Jason would be at the party; Jason was now married with two children. Jean and Larry would be there as well. To honor us, Paco was planning to catch a rabbit, and kill and cook it in front of us; a tradition that I had disliked even as a kid in California. Paco would serenade us, and everyone would come out to participate in the music, drink, and marijuana.

We drove the scenic route to Redway, meandering through the Redwood forests. I gasped at the awesome sights, gazing around at the several hundred foot high trees and dense forests. It was dark, but we stopped on the side of the road to climb atop a fallen down Redway. It was a workout to hoist myself up onto the crumbly trunk; I held my arms up in the air as my dad clicked his camera.

I missed the kids, but Brooks understood when I explained why I had to do the trip now. "I just have to see it. I know being there will help me make my decision. It's all I can think of these days, comparing our life to my childhood. I need to relive that time for a couple of days, and the only way to do it is by going there." I didn't think Brooks completely understood why it was so important to actually be there, but he was sympathetic and said I should do whatever I had to do to confidently make a decision.

Steve was a welcome personality from the high paced crowd I was used to. He and his wife lived in a modest home they were immensely proud of. He walked us through the two bedroom sparsely furnished home as though it was a mansion. He spoke with long pauses, stopping to think carefully before he said a word. I instantly felt like I was on a different planet, and rather than being irritated by his slow pace, it quickly put me at ease. Steve pulled out piles of art books, walking us through his current passion. Steve had not even graduated from high school, but to hear him speak about the intricacies of the art he showed us, I would have thought he had a PhD in art history. He continued to speak slowly and carefully, explaining the themes of various paintings.

"Yola, do you remember when you lived here, you set the record for most books taken out of the library?" Steve placed his hand on my shoulder. "You were one of the most curious kids I've ever met, and Carl here would find books that helped to answer all of your questions."

I thought of Kyle and Ashley, and the inquisitive stage they had just entered. "Mommy, why is the moon white?" "Mommy, how big is the earth?" They loved to ask question after question as we drove around town in the car. I often thought of checking out library books to better answer some of their questions, but I invariably never had enough time. The library was only open during the week, and closed at five p.m; it was impossible for me to ever make it home before five.

"Your dad was quite the character when you lived here," he added. "He would wear that red and black flannel shirt every darn day. You guys were quite the memorable couple; Carl in his shirt, and you holding his hand, skipping along as you always did. I smiled, visualizing us walking hand in hand, remembering our daily trips to the library. I loved to take walks in town with the kids on my Friday's home, but had been increasingly busy with work, and had returned to keeping Linda later and later on Fridays.

We had a light dinner and I said good night to spend some time by myself. My dad had agreed to sleep on the couch, assuming he and Steve would stay up most of the night reminiscing. Steve had begun to ask me about my life in Boston, and I had surprised myself with my openness and honestly. I poured out all my regrets and fears on both Steve and my dad; sharing with the two of them things I had not yet even told my dad. Eventually, I was exhausted, and only wanted to lie in a bed by myself. I shifted uncomfortably on Steve's old mattress; several springs were popping through, and I had to be careful not to roll onto them. I thought of Brooks, lying alone at home in our ultra plush pillow top mattress. I thought of Kyle and Ashley, in the room they shared with their brand new twin beds, and Kaden, probably fast asleep underneath the Mozart mobile that hung above his bed. I was embarrassed to miss the comforts of our fancy home. I had never cared about such material things growing up, and Kyle and Ashley were already demanding the best of the best. I was working hard, making a lot of money, so I could give them everything they deserved. But for what? So they could grow up unable to deal with uncomfortable mattresses? So they could grow up only seeing their mom on the weekends? I tried hard not to impart my stress onto my kids, but it was often impossible; our lives were too hectic. I eventually faded off into the darkness, smelling the familiar smell of marijuana in the air.

We spent time by the river the next day, taking more pictures to remember our visit, and skipping rocks for old times sake. Carl beat me as always. I was surprised to see the homeless still living along the riverbanks. It was a new crew of people, but they hardly looked different. A group was huddled around a campfire, with trash strewn all around their site.

We had a large pancake breakfast at the café in town; a treat that we had only done on rare occasions when we lived there. The homemade sweet potato pancakes were amazing, stuffed with chunks of sweetened potato. My dad took pictures of me walking through town, pretending to be part of the pro-marijuana march that was parading down the street. We laughed at how little had changed in all the years we had been gone. But so much had changed in our lives.

Paco's party was a continuation of our wonderful trip. I felt instantly at ease around the many people I had not seen in twenty-five years. Most of them I barely remembered, but past images were sparked when friends started passing old photographs. A picture of me and Jason, with our arms around each other at age five, almost made me cry. We spent the night sitting on Paco's floor listening to him sing Spanish love songs. I drank too much wine, and almost fell asleep leaning against his couch on the floor. I was happy to be back in Redway, surrounded by friends who had shared in such a significant part of my life. The environment was relaxing and carefree, a stark contrast to the life I led in Boston. A part of me longed to be back in Redway. I wanted my kids to experience so much of what we had there – a carefree life without material things, without nannies, and without business trips.

# Chapter 17 – The next stage of life

I was happier than I'd been in a long time, smiling the whole flight back from Redway. I knew I had to do it, and well before I made anything final, I felt an odd sense of peace.

"Kiddo, that was a great trip. Thank you for the best birthday gift ever." My dad patted me on the shoulder as we said our good-byes, parting ways at Kennedy airport. My dad didn't know yet that the trip had been more of a gift for me. I remembered Meow, my seventh birthday gift, and the lasting impression she had in one short year with us. But Redway, and our six years there, would ultimately have a life long impact on both my children and me.

Although I no longer needed it, the final justification I needed to become just a mom happened shortly after returning from Redway.

"Brooks, I have something to tell you. This is serious."

Brooked looked at me, scared by my tone of voice and facial expression. I rarely was so formal in suggesting the need for a serious discussion. My emotions usually got the best of me, and I was quick to pour my heart out at the most inopportune times. We settled onto the couch, Brooks looking at me with fear and concern in his eyes.

I took a deep breath. I'd been preparing for days how to break the news to him. I was scared of his reaction, but at the same time, felt a sense of confidence that everything would be okay.

"I don't know how it happened…" I paused again, unable to say the words.

Brooks took my hand, his voice trembling as he spoke, "Whatever it is, we can get through it. We've been through so much, and I'm here for you no matter what."

I looked around our comfortable family room, pictures of the kids adorning the mantle, shelves above the television, and on both end tables. I was obsessed with pictures, and wanted to make up for the very few pictures I had as a child. Kyle and Ashley had recently turned three, and the picture collage I always made on their birthday was still tacked to the wall. Kaden had taken his first steps the other day, and I had recently put up a picture of him beaming as he walked unaided down the street. I had the three children I always wanted, and despite feeling overwhelmed, was already excited for what lay ahead of us. I turned, looking Brooks in the eyes, "I'm pregnant."

———∿∿———

My pros and cons of leaving work list had grown longer and longer. I had always been the type of person to act on my instincts, and make decisions too quickly. But this time my instincts had been failing me, and I had been paralyzed by my incessant analysis of the situation. I was done talking it through with Brooks; I had discussed the situation with every friend.

I finally asked myself one question: if I don't' quit work and give the role of full-time mom a chance, will I regret it? I thought of the future; what if one of the kids turned out to have behavioral issues? What if they were behind academically? Would I regret not having been there for them all the time? Framed this way, it was easy to answer yes to my question;

I would regret never taking the risk to put my career aside and devote the time to my children. I asked the question a different way: if I quit work and my long-term career standing ultimately suffered, would I regret doing so for my kids? I found the question phrased this way more difficult to answer. I was a mom now; didn't I owe it to my kids to put their lives first for a while? They clearly needed and wanted me around more often; there was no question about it. That need was finite; they would eventually grow up, and the opportunity would be gone. Work would always be there. I was still torn, but I had come to accept that there was no right answer, and I needed something to rest my final decision on. I made it on my regret question, there was no doubt I would regret not ever giving it a chance. After three years of analyzing, and struggling between career and family, it finally came to me one afternoon.

I quit work the next day. It was time to give my kids some of what my dad had given me: the devoted time and attention they deserved. Arden Madison was born six months later, a healthy baby girl. Kyle, Ashley, Kaden, and Arden were happy to have their mom at home.